MAE
JEMISON

MAE JEMISON

❧

LeeAnne Gelletly

CHELSEA HOUSE PUBLISHERS
Philadelphia

Chelsea House Publishers

Editor in Chief   Sally Cheney
Director of Production   Kim Shinners
Creative Manager   Takeshi Takahashi
Manufacturing Manager   Diann Grasse

Staff for MAE JEMISON

Assistant Editor   Susan Naab
Production Assistant   Jaimie Winkler
Picture Researcher   Sarah Bloom
Series Designer   Takeshi Takahashi
Cover Designer   Terry Mallon
Layout   21st Century Publishing and Communications

The Chelsea House World Wide Web address is
http://www.chelseahouse.com

First Printing

1 3 5 7 9 8 6 4 2

Library of Congress Cataloging-in-Publication Data

Gelletly, LeeAnne.
    Mae Jemison / LeeAnne Gelletly.
       p. cm. — (Black Americans of Achievement)
Summary: A biography of Dr. Mae Jemison who, in September of 1992, on the
fiftieth mission of the United States Space Shuttle, became the first African
American woman in space.
Includes bibliographical references and index.
    ISBN 0-7910-6293-7 (hardback)
  1. Jemison, Mae, 1956- —Juvenile literature. 2. African American women
astronauts—Biography—Juvenile literature. 3. Astronauts—United States—
Biography—Juvenile literature. [1. Jemison, Mae, 1956- 2. Astronauts.
3. African Americans—Biography. 4. Women—Biography.] I. Title. II. Series.
TL789.85.J46 G45 2002
629.45'0092—dc21
                                                                    2002000342

CONTENTS

BLACK AMERICANS OF ACHIEVEMENT

HENRY AARON
baseball great

KAREEM ABDUL-JABBAR
basketball great

MUHAMMAD ALI
heavyweight champion

RICHARD ALLEN
religious leader and social activist

MAYA ANGELOU
author

LOUIS ARMSTRONG
musician

ARTHUR ASHE
tennis great

JOSEPHINE BAKER
entertainer

TYRA BANKS
model

BENJAMIN BANNEKER
scientist and mathematician

COUNT BASIE
bandleader and composer

ANGELA BASSETT
actress

ROMARE BEARDEN
artist

HALLE BERRY
actress

MARY MCLEOD BETHUNE
educator

GEORGE WASHINGTON CARVER
botanist

JOHNNIE COCHRAN
lawyer

BILL COSBY
entertainer

MILES DAVIS
musician

FREDERICK DOUGLASS
abolitionist editor

CHARLES DREW
physician

PAUL LAURENCE DUNBAR
poet

DUKE ELLINGTON
bandleader and composer

RALPH ELLISON
author

JULIUS ERVING
basketball great

LOUIS FARRAKHAN
political activist

ELLA FITZGERALD
singer

ARETHA FRANKLIN
entertainer

MORGAN FREEMAN
actor

MARCUS GARVEY
black nationalist leader

JOSH GIBSON
baseball great

WHOOPI GOLDBERG
entertainer

DANNY GLOVER
actor

CUBA GOODING JR.
actor

ALEX HALEY
author

PRINCE HALL
social reformer

JIMI HENDRIX
musician

MATTHEW HENSON
explorer

GREGORY HINES
performer

BILLIE HOLIDAY
singer

LENA HORNE
entertainer

WHITNEY HOUSTON
singer and actress

LANGSTON HUGHES
poet

JANET JACKSON
musician

JESSE JACKSON
civil-rights leader and politician

MICHAEL JACKSON
entertainer

SAMUEL L. JACKSON
actor

T. D. JAKES
religious leader

JACK JOHNSON *heavyweight champion*	MALCOLM X *militant black leader*	QUEEN LATIFAH *entertainer*	NAT TURNER *slave revolt leader*
MAE JEMISON *astronaut*	BOB MARLEY *musician*	DELLA REESE *entertainer*	TINA TURNER *entertainer*
MAGIC JOHNSON *basketball great*	THURGOOD MARSHALL *Supreme Court justice*	PAUL ROBESON *singer and actor*	ALICE WALKER *author*
SCOTT JOPLIN *composer*	TERRY MCMILLAN *author*	JACKIE ROBINSON *baseball great*	MADAM C. J. WALKER *entrepreneur*
BARBARA JORDAN *politician*	TONI MORRISON *author*	CHRIS ROCK *comedian and actor*	BOOKER T. WASHINGTON *educator*
MICHAEL JORDAN *basketball great*	ELIJAH MUHAMMAD *religious leader*	DIANA ROSS *entertainer*	DENZEL WASHINGTON *actor*
CORETTA SCOTT KING *civil-rights leader*	EDDIE MURPHY *entertainer*	AL SHARPTON *minister and activist*	J. C. WATTS *politician*
MARTIN LUTHER KING, JR. *civil-rights leader*	JESSE OWENS *champion athlete*	WILL SMITH *actor*	VANESSA WILLIAMS *singer and actress*
LEWIS LATIMER *scientist*	SATCHEL PAIGE *baseball great*	WESLEY SNIPES *actor*	VENUS WILLIAMS *tennis star*
SPIKE LEE *filmmaker*	CHARLIE PARKER *musician*	CLARENCE THOMAS *Supreme Court justice*	OPRAH WINFREY *entertainer*
CARL LEWIS *champion athlete*	ROSA PARKS *civil-rights leader*	SOJOURNER TRUTH *antislavery activist*	TIGER WOODS *golf star*
RONALD MCNAIR *astronaut*	COLIN POWELL *military leader*	HARRIET TUBMAN *antislavery activist*	

ON
ACHIEVEMENT

— ❧ —

Coretta Scott King

Before you begin this book, I hope you will ask yourself what the word *excellence* means to you. I think it's a question we should all ask, and keep asking as we grow older and change. Because the truest answer to it should never change. When you think of excellence, perhaps you think of success at work; or of becoming wealthy; or meeting the right person, getting married, and having a good family life.

Those goals are worth striving for, but there is a better way to look at excellence. As Martin Luther King Jr. said in one of his last sermons, "I want you to be first in love. I want you to be first in moral excellence. I want you to be first in generosity. If you want to be important, wonderful. If you want to be great, wonderful. But recognize that he who is greatest among you shall be your servant."

My husband knew that the true meaning of achievement is service. When I met him, in 1952, he was already ordained as a Baptist minister and was working toward a doctoral degree at Boston University. I was studying at the New England Conservatory and dreamed of accomplishments in music. We married a year later, and after I graduated the following year we moved to Montgomery, Alabama. We didn't know it then, but our notions of achievement were about to undergo a dramatic change.

You may have read or heard about what happened next. What began with the boycott of a local bus line grew into a national crusade, and by the time he was assassinated in 1968 my husband had fashioned a black movement powerful enough to shatter forever the practice of racial segregation. What you may not have read about is where he learned to resist injustice without compromising his religious beliefs.

He adopted a strategy of nonviolence from a man of a different race, who lived in a different country and even practiced a different religion. The man was Mahatma Gandhi, the great leader of India, who devoted his life to serving humanity in the spirit of love and nonviolence. It was in these principles that Martin discovered his method for social reform. More than anything else, those two principles were the key to his achievements.

These books are about African Americans who served society through the excellence of their achievements. They form part of the rich history of black men and women in America—a history of stunning accomplishments in every field of human endeavor, from literature and art to science, industry, education, diplomacy, athletics, jurisprudence, even polar exploration.

Not all of the people in this history had the same ideals, but I think you will find that all of them had something in common. Like Martin Luther King Jr., they all decided to become "drum majors" and serve humanity. In that principle—whether it was expressed in books, inventions, or song—they found a goal and a guide outside themselves that showed them a way to serve others instead of living only for themselves.

Reading the stories of these courageous men and women not only helps us discover the principles that we will use to guide our own lives; it also teaches us about our black heritage and about America itself. It is crucial for us to know the heroes and heroines of our history and to realize that the price we paid in our struggle for equality in America was dear. But we must also understand that we have gotten as far as we have partly because America's democratic system and ideals made it possible.

We are still struggling with racism and prejudice. But the great men and women in this series are a tribute to the spirit of the country in which they have flourished. And that makes their stories special and worth knowing.

1

"TO BOLDLY GO ..."

❦

IN THE EARLY morning hours of Saturday, September 12, 1992, seven astronauts clad in bright orange space suits stood at launch pad 39-B at the Kennedy Space Center in Florida. More than 30 stories above them loomed the three main components of the space shuttle: the sleek white orbiter—the *Endeavour*—nestled between its two solid-fuel rocket boosters and joined to a huge rust-colored external fuel tank. One member of the *Endeavour*'s crew, a tall, 35-year-old African American woman with short-cropped black hair and sparkling brown eyes, gazed at the massive space shuttle with special excitement. Dr. Mae Carol Jemison was poised to fulfill the dream of a lifetime.

Mae was about to embark on the 50th mission of the U.S. space shuttle and would soon join the elite corps of astronauts who had journeyed into orbit. With this flight, Jemison would become a part of history as well, for she was about to become the first African American woman in space.

The U.S. space shuttle program had been in existence for more than a decade, having flown its first mission in 1981. Unlike the spacecraft developed during the early years of the National Aeronautics and Space Administration (NASA)—the U.S. space agency—the shuttle could be used

Mae Jemison poses with her fellow crewmembers prior to the historic 1992 launch of the shuttle Endeavour. *Front row (from left to right): Jerome Apt, mission specialist; Curtis Brown, pilot; Back row (from left to right): J. Nan Davis, mission specialist; Mark Lee, payload commander; Robert Gibson, mission commander; Mae Jemison; and Mamoru Mohri, payload specialist.*

11

for missions again and again. Because of this feature, NASA could fund many more missions and schedule far more flights into space than had ever been possible during the 1960s and '70s. Besides the *Endeavour,* three other orbiters—the *Discovery, Atlantis,* and *Columbia*—now regularly traveled to the stars. The space shuttle, which launched like a rocket and landed like a plane, had flown hundreds of astronauts into space and then safely returned them to Earth. But until today, none of these astronauts had been a woman of color.

Preparations for the Saturday launch had been slowed the day before because of the threat of severe thunderstorms near the Kennedy Space Center launch site. Nevertheless, technicians had managed to prepare the *Endeavour* for its week-long research mission, loading the orbiter with the animals—two carp, four frogs, thousands of fruit fly larvae, and one hundred eighty hornets—that were to be used in experiments aboard the space shuttle.

By early Saturday morning, the weather had cleared and launch procedures were on schedule. The seven *Endeavour* astronauts entered the mid-deck of the orbiter's crew cabin and climbed into their seats, which, since the orbiter stood in an upright position, required them to lie on their backs. The *Endeavour*'s commander, Robert L. "Hoot" Gibson, and pilot, Curtis L. Brown Jr., climbed up to their seats on the flight deck. They sat above the rest of the crew, who were strapped into seats beneath, two on the flight deck and the other three astronauts in the mid-deck of the cabin.

Finally, the launch countdown came to an end, and at 10:23 A.M. Eastern Daylight Time, the 78-ton *Endeavour* lifted off right on schedule and ascended into the bright blue Florida sky. During the next eight minutes, approximately 781,400 pounds of thrust powered the shuttle up to a speed of more than 17,000 miles per hour, about nine times as fast as a rifle bullet.

The shuttle's northern course took it along the East Coast of the United States. Two minutes after launch, the solid rocket boosters separated from the orbiter and external tank, and parachuted to the Atlantic Ocean to be retrieved for reuse. About eight minutes into the flight, after pushing the *Endeavour* into space, the external tank, now empty, separated from the shuttle, breaking up and burning as it reentered the Earth's atmosphere.

Mae recalled the physical effect caused by the force of liftoff: "It takes about eight minutes to get from the Kennedy Space Center into orbit. During the last four minutes, you feel a lot of pressure across your chest. You feel like you weigh about three times what you weigh on Earth." But her emotional reaction at liftoff overwhelmed her much more. In an interview with *Ebony* magazine, she remembered the exhilaration she felt as the *Endeavour* rose with a roar toward the heavens: "I had this big smile on my face. I was so excited. This is what I had wanted to do for a very long time. . . . It was the realization of many, many dreams of many people."

At almost 260 miles above the Earth, the *Endeavour* was moved into a circular orbit, with its tail pointed toward the planet. This position allowed for optimal radio communication with ground control and placed the orbiter so its equipment would generate heat out toward space. The *Endeavour* would be traveling in a 17,500 mile-per-hour orbit around Earth, circling the Earth every 90 minutes. Its route would reach as far north as Moscow, in Russia, and as far south as the tip of South America.

On a beautiful Florida morning the Endeavour *and her crew leave the launch pad and rocket into a clear blue sky. The powerful engines must push the* Endeavour *to nearly 17,000 miles per hour to reach orbit.*

Once a spaceship establishes orbit, it is in a state of continuous "free fall" around the planet. Gravity still pulls on the spacecraft, but because it is flying away from the Earth at the same rate that gravity is trying to pull it back down, weightlessness occurs. Anything not secured inside the orbiter will float as if it has no weight. After the *Endeavour* established orbit, its crew members unfastened their safety restraints and set to work, floating about as they attended to their tasks.

Mission specialist Mae Jemison was still stowing away the orange suits the astronauts had worn for launch when Commander "Hoot" Gibson called her to the front of the orbiter. As she reached the flight deck, the captain pointed out that they were passing over a very familiar place to Mae—the city of Chicago. She remembers seeing the city as a contrast of gray-colored concrete buildings set against the lush greens of the farmland surrounding it. As the shuttle sped along in its orbit, that view—her first from space—vanished within minutes.

In later interviews, Mae described her first impressions of the sights she saw from space. In one interview with *People Weekly*, she described the vibrant colors visible from her perch on the *Endeavour*: "The earth was gorgeous. There was a blue iridescent glow about the planet that was tremendous."

But there was more than just the beauty of the images before her. Aboard the *Endeavour*, Mae also felt a sense of satisfaction, of having arrived somewhere where she belonged, of having come home at last. She explained the experience: "Looking down and all around me, seeing the earth, the moon, and the stars, I felt just like I belonged right here, and in fact any place in the entire universe. And I had known since I was seven years old that the universe was a very big place."

THE STAR TREK CONNECTION

"Huntsville, Endeavour. All hailing frequencies open." Dr. Mae Jemison smiled to herself as she repeated these words. The tall, brown-eyed African American woman was at the beginning of her shift aboard the space shuttle *Endeavour*, 260 miles above the Earth, and had broken with the usual protocol by addressing the Marshall Space Flight Center in such a way. Her words echoed those of a fictional character from a long-ago science fiction television program—but with them, the first female African American astronaut was paying tribute to a mentor who had inspired Mae Jemison to journey to the stars.

That mentor was a fictional television character named Lt. Uhura, the elegant, self-assured communications officer of the 1960s television show *Star Trek*. Set in the distant future, *Star Trek* followed the adventures of the crew of the USS *Enterprise* as it traveled the universe on a mission *"to explore strange new worlds and seek out new life and new civilizations. . . . to boldly go where no man has gone before."* Uhura, played by the African American actress Nichelle Nichols, used the phrase *"all hailing frequencies open"* whenever she operated the communications systems for the starship *Enterprise*.

Just 10 years old when the show premiered in 1966, Mae had been impressed by the black woman's presence on the show, when most television programs featured all-white casts. Not only was Uhura, whose name comes from the Kiswahili word for "freedom," a woman in space at a time when only white men were astronauts, but also the lieutenant was African American. Jemison noted in her autobiography that *"[Lt. Uhura] was the first woman to appear regularly on television in a technical role. She was intelligent, skilled, gorgeous, cool, and looked a bit like me and the women around me."* The character inspired the young girl, making it seem that the dream of space travel was possible for Mae, too.

During the 1960s, Mae Jemison had watched television broadcasts of U.S. space efforts. She knew that the Soviet Union had sent a woman cosmonaut, Valentina Tereshkova, into space in 1964, so the thought of her own venture seemed possible. But at the time, the country's space agency—the National Aeronautics and Space Administration (NASA)—chose only military pilots to serve as astronauts, and all were white males.

Then *Star Trek* aired in 1966, and Mae's dream of becoming a star voyager received a boost. She explained in her autobiography, *"When Star Trek premiered, I was only ten years old, but I already knew that I would travel in space. . . . I had defiantly pronounced that NASA and anyone else who tried to explain as reasonable the idea that women were not suited to be astronauts were nonsensical."* She was not about to be limited by anyone else, she added. *"I had already decided that I would go into space. The fact that all the U.S. astronauts then were white men just made it a little more difficult, a challenge."*

Boldly going where no African-American woman had gone before, Jemison echoed the words of *Star Trek*'s Lt. Uhura (shown here in a photo from the 1960s TV show) as she declared "all hailing frequencies open" on the 50th mission of the U.S. space shuttle.

2

DREAMING OF THE STARS

Born in Alabama, Jemison moved with her family to Chicago when she was three. There, her mother earned both a bachelor's and master's degree in education, while her father worked as a maintenance supervisor and part-time construction worker.

ALTHOUGH MAE JEMISON considers Chicago, Illinois, her hometown, the southern city of Decatur, Alabama, is her actual birthplace. When she was born, on October 17, 1956, the small town of Decatur consisted of about 30,000 citizens. Located in the northern part of the state, Decatur lies close to Huntsville, Alabama—now the site of the Marshall Space Flight Center, a place where the future astronaut would spend a great deal of time.

Mae Jemison was the youngest child of Dorothy and Charlie Jemison, who already had one son, Ricky, and a daughter, Ada Sue. Although not financially well-off, both Dorothy and Charlie were prepared to give their children the love, support, and education they needed to do well in life.

Dorothy had grown up in Florence, Alabama, and was the adopted daughter of John and Ada Green. When she turned 18, Dorothy Green began college at one of the oldest black universities in the country, Talladega College, located in Talladega, Alabama. Charlie Jemison's parents, Primus and Susie Jemison, were from the same Alabama town, and Charlie met Dorothy at a college dance there.

When Dorothy's parents became ill, the young student left school without completing her education so she could take care of them. Later, after she and Charlie married, the couple took up residence

19

in one side of a two-family duplex in Decatur. There Charlie took work as a roofer and carpenter. While the three Jemison children were young, Dorothy stayed at home to care for them, although she occasionally took jobs cleaning houses and sewing clothes.

When Mae was three and a half years old, Dorothy Jemison decided that she had to find a better way of life for herself and her family. Because she believed that the North offered better work and educational opportunities for her and the children, she packed up her family and traveled with them by train to Chicago, Illinois. Dorothy had not been happy with the jobs available in Decatur; despite having two years of college, the only work she had been able to find was cleaning houses. Mae recalls that the move was especially difficult because her father stayed behind in Alabama. Her mother had been determined to leave Decatur, and had left on her own.

A few months after the move, Charlie Jemison followed his family to Illinois. There he found work as a maintenance supervisor at United Charities of Chicago and as a part-time construction worker. The family settled in an apartment in the Woodlawn section, on the south side of inner-city Chicago.

In Chicago, Dorothy found what she was looking for, for both herself and her children. She earned her bachelor's degree in education and then found work as a schoolteacher at the Beethoven Elementary School in the Robert Taylor Homes projects. A few years later, she added a master's degree to her résumé. Mae notes that seeing her mother go back to school while raising three children was "an enduring lesson in perseverance and lifelong learning," one that made a lasting impression on her.

Life soon fell into a routine. While Mae's mother took college courses, Charlie Jemison took care of the family, fixing meals, braiding Mae's hair, and getting her ready for school. Charlie and Dorothy worked while Mae went to nursery school. Mae admits she was proud that, unlike most of the other children at her school, her mother worked while the other mothers did not.

When she was five, Mae entered McCosh Elementary School. Even in kindergarten, Mae was a strong-minded child who wasn't afraid to be different or to stand up for herself. She often tells others about one incident in school that reflected who she is today: Each member of the kindergarten class was asked what he or she wanted to be when grown up. The other children in the class responded with cries of "fireman," "teacher," or "mother." However, Mae had a different idea. She announced that she planned to become a scientist when she grew up.

To the kindergarten teacher, the goal of a young African American girl to become a scientist must have seemed unrealistic in the early 1960s. With a look of puzzled dismay, she attempted to correct the young girl, "Don't you mean a nurse?" Not at all discouraged by her teacher's negative reaction, Mae insisted that she meant to become a scientist. Even at the age of five, she knew she could be exactly what she wanted to be in life. When Mae relates this story to others, she often refers to it as an example of how individuals must refuse to be limited by others' "limited imagination."

From an early age, Mae was drawn to science. She particularly liked anthropology (the study of the origin and development of people), archaeology (the study of ancient civilization), astronomy (the study of the planets and stars), and evolution (the theory that groups of organisms change physiologically over the course of time). Her parents encouraged her interest in science by encouraging

The wonder of a spiral galaxy. Mae expressed an interest in science, including astronomy, as early as age five, announcing her ambition to be a scientist to her kindergarten class.

her to read, study, and ask questions. To help feed her driving desire to learn more about the world, they took her on trips to city museums, such as the Museum of Science and Industry and the Field Museum of Natural History.

Along with exposing their young daughter to extra educational opportunities, Mae's parents encouraged her to learn to think for herself. Mae credits her mother with teaching her to take initiative for learning on her own. Whenever Mae would ask her mother a question about something that interested her, Dorothy Jemison would reply, "Look it up." In this way, Mae believes, she learned the importance of research and self-reliance, as she recalled in a 1996 interview with *Stanford Today*: "My mother always told me to go find out the information myself. She was very directive, in the sense of 'it's your responsibility,' sort of like those people who tell you to go look up a word in the dictionary when you don't know how to spell it."

In the interview, she also mentions her Uncle Louis, a social worker, who helped foster her interest in science at an early age. Already a curious and questioning child, Mae appreciated that her uncle took the time to talk to her about her interests in the stars and in the space program. Because he believed her capable of understanding scientific concepts such as the size and distance of the stars, she grew up believing she could understand anything and was inspired to learn all she could.

Mae has fond memories of childhood adventures with her older brother and sister, Ricky and Ada Sue. As the youngest, she would usually be the target of whatever teasing they doled out or the one following them into whatever escapades they led her on. As an adult, she admits that the lure of being with her older siblings gave her courage to try things she might otherwise have avoided. "Even if I was frightened, I was still 'game' if it meant I could hang with the older kids," she noted in her autobiography.

When Mae turned eight years old, her mother decided that dance classes would help her young daughter overcome some of her childhood clumsiness. At first, Mae was enrolled in beginning ballet classes at the Sadie Bruce Dance Academy. To get to these lessons, Mae had to take the Chicago El train (an aboveground subway train) all by herself, a journey she undertook every Saturday morning. It was a fearful experience, not because she traveled alone but because she had to walk up the steps to the El platform, and at the time she was very afraid of heights.

The following year Dorothy enrolled Mae in modern dance classes with Michelle Madison at the Jane Addams Hull House Association Community Center. Mae recalled how the discipline of modern dance classes helped her:

> Every Saturday morning Mrs. Madison would work us very hard with basic dance movements, techniques, and exercises. . . . We would learn complicated dance routines that always challenged me to understand shape, form, and rhythm. . . . I grew stronger with [Mrs. Madison]. I gained an appreciation for hard work, physical strength, and grace that has stayed with me through the years.

The Jemison family lived in the all-black Wood-lawn neighborhood of Chicago for seven years. But as the children grew up, the area came to hold more dangers, especially for young African American males. Stories of gang fights, stabbings, and shootings became commonplace. One warm summer evening, as the Jemison children sat with their friends on the front stoop of their first-floor apartment, Mae's brother, Ricky, was confronted by members of a gang known as the Blackstone Rangers.

Before the situation could escalate beyond harsh words and name-calling, Mae's mother came to the doorway. She had been warned of the trouble by one of the neighborhood boys who had slipped away into the apartment. With a pistol grasped in her hand, Dorothy Jemison demanded that the gang leave. Because Mae and her sister hadn't thought to warn

When Mae was nine, her mother enrolled her in modern dance classes, where she gained an appreciation for strength, form, and rhythm. Years later, she took lessons at the Alvin Ailey Dance Studio in New York City. Here, Ailey poses with two members of his dance company.

their mother about what was happening, they were punished. As Mae later explained, "This had been a very dangerous and volatile situation, we should have informed [our mother]. We already knew that if one of us ever got into a fight we were expected, no required, to help out. It didn't matter how big the other kids were. But we were also expected to use good judgement and get someone who could help."

Soon afterward, the Jemison family left Woodlawn

and moved to Morgan Park, becoming the first black family on the block of the far south-side Chicago neighborhood. Although the high school was integrated at the time, the neighborhood was not. That fall Mae entered the mostly white Esmond Elementary School—although she was the age of a seventh grader, administrators placed her in the eighth grade because her test scores indicated she could do the work required of seniors in high school. At Esmond she took advanced classes in math, science, and reading.

Reading had long been one of Mae's favorite activities because it helped her learn about whatever interested her. When she was 10, her sixth-grade class had studied the constellations. At that time Mae had developed a powerful urge to learn as much as she could about the stars and astronomy—the universe, the planets, and galaxies, and even the Greek myths and stories used to name so many heavenly bodies. "I was and remain absolutely fascinated by the stars, planets, and universe," she later recalled. "I always wanted to know more about cosmology, physics, theories on how the universe was formed, and what stars were made of. I learned about most of this by reading on my own." She often found the books she wanted by frequenting the local library of Woodlawn and, later, Morgan Park.

Mae didn't read only science books, however. She also enjoyed fiction, particularly science fiction. She notes that the first science fiction book that "hooked" her was written by Fred Hoyle, a British astronomer who wrote *A for Andromeda* (Andromeda is the name of the galaxy closest to Earth's own Milky Way Galaxy). The list of other favorite science fiction authors later included Isaac Asimov and Arthur C. Clarke. Mae once analyzed her fascination with the genre: "Inside of each science fiction book I saw the hope that humans would do better, that we could advance. Mystery and adversity challenged our character. I found imagination, fantasy, and possibilities between the pages. Interestingly, as a young black woman, I identified with grown white men who were the main characters and heroes. I identified with the desire to understand the world."

Although most of these books did not feature women as strong role models or members of minority groups as scientists, the young reader found she could overlook the omissions. However, she eventually did discover and devour books by other science fiction and adventure authors, such as Octavia Butler, Marion Zimmer Bradley, Anne McCaffrey, and Madeleine L'Engle, who included women and minorities as main characters.

As Mae grew up during the 1960s, she developed a strong understanding of her own heritage as an African American. Her parents made sure that she learned about blacks who were inventors, athletes, and scholars. Her mother and father also engaged their children in discussions around the kitchen table about politics. They talked of problems in U.S. society, and the ongoing civil rights movement, in which blacks were struggling to obtain legal, educational, and social equality with whites.

Some groups in the civil rights movement, like the Black Panther Party, advocated violence to achieve their goals. When Mae was 10 years old, racial tensions in the United States fueled riots that rocked the city of Chicago, as well as cities across the nation. A year later, in the spring of 1968, destruction came close to Mae's own neighborhood during the Democratic National Convention. Just blocks away from her home, stores were looted and burned. In response, city officials imposed curfews and members of the National Guard patrolled Chicago. In her autobiography, Mae recalled the terror she felt when she

Mae grew up during a turbulent time in U.S. political history. The 1968 Democratic National Convention in Chicago spurred riots between anti-war demonstrators and National Guard troops. Despite the violence so near her home, Mae vowed not to live in fear.

saw National Guardsmen marching with rifles in the streets outside her home:

> I was so scared. . . . Children as young as thirteen had been shot and killed during the riots. . . . These adults, these representatives, enforcers of the United States government would hold me in suspicion and probably shoot me if I was out on the street. So I cowered behind the back door screen to see who they were. They looked like regular folk—but ready for war.

But Mae was angry too, and at that time made a promise to herself that she would never again be so frightened by the events of her world. She was a citizen of the United States and had rights, too, and, as she noted in her autobiography, she also had a "responsibility to work to help our country to fulfill its promise." This attitude would affect many decisions she would make in the future.

Because Mae had been advanced a grade, she was just 12 years old when she entered Morgan Park High School, which in 1969 was an integrated school located just a few blocks from her home. During Mae's freshman year, both Ricky and Ada Sue were also at Morgan Park, which had a reputation as a college prep school attended by kids from middle-class families.

Mae enjoyed herself tremendously at high school, where she participated in many extracurricular activities. She became a member of the pom-pon squad during her freshman and sophomore years; served as president of the modern dance club; and participated in ballet and dance classes, science fairs, and plays. She was president of the Russian club, and during her senior year tested wills occasionally with administrators while serving as student council president.

Mae especially liked classes in art and archaeology, but she also excelled academically in the sciences—biology, physics, and chemistry. She remembers being the first girl to sign up for drafting class at her high school, a traditionally male-oriented course involving the drawing of plans and sketches of machinery and structures. She had wanted to take the class because of a growing interest in architecture and engineering.

As Dorothy Jemison raised her three outgoing children, she applied the same principles she brought to teaching—the belief that children learn best when self-directed. As she grew up, Mae knew that whenever she wanted to learn about something, she had to take on the responsibility of learning about it on her own. When Mae was a junior at Morgan Park High, she had the exceptional experience of doing "hands-on" research on sickle-cell anemia. After asking her mother what sickle-cell anemia was, she had received the expected response: find out about it on your own. So Mae set out to do just that.

Soon the curious student learned that sickle-cell anemia is an inherited disease of the blood commonly found in people of African ancestry. The illness causes severe pain and is usually fatal by the time the afflicted person reaches his or her twenties. The name comes from the shape of the red blood cells, which, because of the disease, are shaped like sickles instead of circles—the shape of healthy red blood cells.

To learn more about sickle-cell anemia, Mae decided to visit the Cook County Hospital, a major institution on the West Side of Chicago. To get there from her home on the South Side, Mae had to take both the train and bus, and the teen took pride in being able to figure out how to make the trip on her own.

At the hospital's hematology lab, which did research on blood and blood-forming organs, Mae met several people who helped her learn more about sickle-cell anemia. She ended up working in the hematology labs each week for the next several months. During that time she learned how to test for sickle-cell anemia, how it is diagnosed, and, more important, how to set up a scientific experiment to evaluate compounds that could inhibit the disease. Under the guidance of the head of the hematology department, Mae developed a project that she ultimately submitted in the City Wide Chicago Public School Science Fair, where it received high honors.

Dorothy Jemison had been correct in believing that the city of Chicago would provide her children with many educational opportunities and valuable experiences. But she and Charlie Jemison also provided the strong foundation and encouragement their children needed to succeed to the best of their talents and abilities. Mae's sister, Ada Jemison Bullock, went on to attend medical school and become a child psychiatrist. Her brother, Ricky Jemison, found work as a real estate broker. Mae attributes her own success to the overwhelming support of her parents, who encouraged her ambitions and helped her develop and maintain self-confidence. As she explained in a 1989 interview with *Ebony* magazine: "My parents have always been supportive of me. When I was a child, they put up with all kinds of stuff, like science projects, dance classes and art lessons. They encouraged me to do it, and they would find the money, time and energy to help me be involved."

Mae worked hard throughout high school, and her name appeared consistently on the honor roll. In 1973, at the age of 16, she graduated from Morgan Park High School with great plans for her future. Because of the high scores she had earned on Preliminary Scholastic Aptitude Tests (PSATs), Mae received a National Achievement Scholarship that paid her university tuition. She received scholarship offers from Massachusetts Institute of Technology, Rensselaer Polytechnic Institute, Bell Labs, and Stanford University. After careful consideration, she chose a college she knew would provide what she wanted, although it was located far from home. Still, she eagerly looked forward to the new opportunities to explore at Stanford University in the San Francisco Bay Area of California.

3

EXPLORING NEW WORLDS

———— ❧ ————

A N EXCITED MAE Jemison stood in the bustling terminal of O'Hare Airport in Chicago, surrounded by luggage crammed with her clothing, much of which she had created and sewn herself. The multitalented teen excelled not only at academics but also at handiwork—after learning to sew by stitching outfits for her Barbie dolls, she had applied the same skills in designing and making her own clothing.

Just 16 years old, Mae was about to set off on a new adventure—ready to board and travel by herself on a plane bound for San Francisco, California, and a future life at Stanford University. It was a scary time. Aware that she was leaving behind beloved family members and friends, Mae was assailed by a range of conflicting emotions. In her autobiography, she recalled how she felt: "I was nervous, excited, lonely, sad, and happy all at the same time." But although two years younger than the typical 18-year-old college freshman, Mae was ready to explore future opportunities.

Upon arriving at Stanford, Mae learned she was housed in a dorm that held freshmen, sophomores, juniors, and seniors—and she was the youngest person in the building. However, her dorm mates thought it was "pretty cool" that someone her age was attending Stanford, and they treated her the

At age 16, Mae enrolled at California's Stanford University, where she studied chemical engineering. It soon became clear that, as an African-American woman, Mae would have to work hard to receive the credit she deserved.

same as everyone else. As a freshman at Stanford, Mae focused immediately on fulfilling the requirements that would earn her a degree in biomedical engineering. A new field at the time, biomedical engineering involves using technology to help treat human diseases; for example, a biomedical engineer might design devices such as an artificial heart or medical monitoring equipment. Between her junior and senior years of high school, while attending a two-week summer program sponsored by the Junior Engineering Technical Society at the University of Illinois in Urbana, Mae had learned about the new science. "That summer I was able to reconcile my love of physics, biology, practical implementation, and creativity in this one area of biomedical engineering," Jemison explained in her autobiography. At Stanford, she would have to pursue studies in biology, physics, and chemistry in order to earn a degree in biomedical engineering.

Mae entered Stanford University with additional goals: to continue learning Russian—a language that she believed would be important in future science research and space exploration—and to become involved in dance and athletics. However, the optimistic new freshman soon found herself uncertain about her ability, and her self-confidence sorely tested by some of her Stanford professors.

Early on, Mae became aware that a few of her teachers seemed to treat her differently than they did many of her other classmates. Up until college, she had often found teachers and advisers who not only encouraged her ambitions but also complimented her on her intelligence and abilities. Yet at Stanford she was taken aback when her first adviser told her that he believed she belonged in beginner's classes, in both mathematics and Russian. Mae had completed advanced mathematics and four years of Russian in high school, but she was too embarrassed to question her adviser's opinion. She ended up dropping Russian completely; however, she did take high-level math classes—calculus and solid analytic geometry—the first quarter of her freshman year, along with courses in introductory chemistry, women's physiology, and English.

In her freshman chemistry class, Mae encountered the same negativism and prejudice she could attribute only to the color of her skin, her gender, or both. She recalled in her autobiography, "[W]hen I would ask questions, Professor Weinhardt would either ignore me, or act as though I was impossibly dumb for not knowing the answer. When a white boy down the row asked the exact same questions, Weinhardt would say 'Very good observation,' and explain." It soon became clear to Mae that, as a female African American, she would have to work harder than most of the other students to receive credit for and recognition of her abilities.

During Mae's first year at Stanford, she decided to follow the guidance of a second adviser, who encouraged her to major in chemical engineering instead of biomedical engineering. Mae was still interested in pursuing a career in this new technology field, but, as her adviser pointed out, the chemical engineering degree was recognized as an established, rigorous program, whereas biomedical engineering was not. And with the chemical engineering degree she could obtain the necessary background to later pursue graduate work in the new field.

As she took the required classes for a chemical engineering degree, Mae also took the opportunity to learn more about herself, specifically her African-American heritage. After deciding to drop Russian, she replaced the class with Swahili, a language used in much of East Africa and the Congo. Her sister, Ada Sue, had also taken Swahili in college, and

Mae wanted to learn more about it. What she liked even more, however, was that the professor who taught the course took an interest in her as a person, something she had not encountered in her science and engineering classes.

When she was not studying, Mae participated in several extracurricular activities, especially those involving theater and dance. She took African and modern dance classes, had a role in the play *No Place to Be Somebody*, and appeared in the musical *Purlie*. Mae ultimately became involved in many other college dance and drama productions, producing and directing shows as well as performing in them. As a representative of the arts for Stanford University, she traveled abroad for the first time in 1976, when she visited Jamaica to participate in its Carifesta, the annual Caribbean Festival of Arts.

Mae admits to another strong interest in college —football. She would later joke that the reason she decided to attend Stanford in 1973 was that the school had had back-to-back football victories at the Rose Bowl in the early 1970s. Not only did Stanford have a winning football team but it also sponsored coed intramural football leagues. Although Mae hadn't played football before, she knew enough about the rules of the game to join a dorm team that included two girls.

After her freshmen year, Mae took many other courses that focused on the history, politics, culture, and languages of Africa. She was especially compelled to learn as much as she could about Africa after participating in a class during her sophomore year called "Politics in Sub-Saharan Africa," taught by David Abernathy.

As she grew more informed about and proud of her African heritage, Mae became involved in activities affecting blacks in present-day America. She served as president of the Black Student Union,

becoming the first female to do so. She also designed and helped teach two classes on racism at Stanford: one entitled "Race and Politics in Education" and the other, "Race and Culture in the Caribbean."

To fulfill the requirements for her engineering degree, Mae took many graduate-level courses, instead of enrolling in undergraduate classes. Some of these more-challenging classes included "Life Science in Space Exploration," "Biomedical Instrumentation," and "Biomedical Fluid Mechanics." These classes required her to work hard, and,

Stanford has long been known for its football program, winning back-to-back Rose Bowls in the 1970s. Mae has joked that she attended the school because of these successful seasons.

although she did well in them, she continued to find that she had to work harder than many of her fellow students to have her abilities recognized. Meanwhile, she discovered, the professors teaching the classes she was taking in African studies—political science, history, linguistics, and language—provided her with the encouragement to believe in herself and in her abilities. Mae fondly recalled how these teachers helped her maintain her self-confidence:

> They believed in me as a student, unlike the feeling I got in most of the engineering and science classes. I did not have to jump over hurdles each time I walked in the door just to prove I belonged there. The social sciences professors were interested in my ideas, insights, and comments. My intelligence was legitimate. Looking back, I realize that it was important for me as a student to have professors who believed in me, teachers who felt that I could become one of their colleagues.

However, Mae also admits that the challenges she faced with some of her less-than-supportive professors also helped make her a stronger person than she had been before.

In 1977 Mae Jemison graduated from Stanford University with a bachelor of science degree in chemical engineering and having fulfilled the requirements for a bachelor of arts degree in African and African American studies. She was not awarded the second degree, however, because Stanford required double-major students to remain at the school an additional year before they could receive the second degree. Even though she did not receive a degree for the work she did in African American studies, Mae believes she benefited tremendously from taking the courses.

Although a gifted science student, she recognized the importance of being knowledgeable in many different areas:

> Science is very important to me, but I also like to stress that you have to be well-rounded. One's love for science doesn't get rid of all the other areas. I truly feel someone interested in science is interested in understanding what's going on in the world. That means you have to find out about social science, art, and politics . . .

Making career choices can be tough. When Mae was young, she had thought about becoming an architect or fashion designer when she grew up. But by the time she graduated from high school, she had decided on becoming a biomedical engineer. Then, during her years at Stanford, she enjoyed theater and dance activities so much that she wasn't so sure about what she wanted to do and, in fact, seriously considered becoming a professional dancer. Still, the desire to work in the field of biomedical engineering pulled even stronger. To best prepare for that career, Mae decided, she needed to apply to medical school. She did not plan to actually practice medicine, Mae has admitted; her long-term goal was to gain the skills needed to do research as a biomedical engineer.

In the fall of 1977 Mae prepared for her next challenge. She had been accepted at Cornell University Medical College, which necessitated a move across the country to New York City. During the 1970s, very few black women were receiving undergraduate degrees in science, and even fewer were being accepted to graduate programs. Mae's accomplishments at this point in her life reflect her great talents and abilities, as well as her focus and determination.

Mae has stated that at medical school she learned how to study and to focus on her work and goals. Still, it took a few weeks before the new medical school student figured out she had to change her work habits. At Stanford she had usually studied just during her free afternoons; at Cornell she had to establish much more disciplined work habits. Before tests, she studied until 2:00 o'clock in the morning; or, if she went to sleep at midnight, she had to wake at 4:30 or 5:00 the next morning in order to continue studying.

Medical school students have to memorize massive amounts of information. In gross anatomy class, for example, where one learns about various parts of the human body (muscles, internal organs, blood vessels, bones, and nerves), Mae needed to be able to name and locate the thousands of different body structures illustrated in her human body atlases, dissection manual, and textbooks. She remembers how, on the very first day of gross anatomy, her instructor directed the students into the lab, where they began dissecting human cadavers. The high demands and expectations of the medical school teachers took some getting used to. Mae's sister Ada Sue, who was in her fourth year of medical school at the time, helped Mae out by providing helpful advice and texts.

Despite the demands of work, Mae still managed to find time for exercise. Whenever possible, she took lessons at the Alvin Ailey Dance Studio and with the Katherine Dunham Troupe, which specialized in African dancing. She and a friend played pickup basketball games in the school gym.

Mae also found time to volunteer in various activities. During her first year at Cornell, she helped prepare a pamphlet on prescription drug abuse for high school students, then visited a local New York high school to distribute the pamphlet

On September 12, 1992, Mae Jemison and her crewmates prepared to embark on their mission as they headed for Launch Complex 39, where they would board the space shuttle Endeavour—only fifteen years after her decision to enter medical school.

and help drive home its message. The following summer she traveled to Cuba with an American Medical Student Association (AMSA) study group.

Mae continued with volunteer activities throughout her years at medical school. During her second year, as president of the Cornell chapter of the Student National Medical Association, she helped organize a combined health and law fair in New York City (with medical students from Cornell, New Jersey Medical and Dental, Einstein, and New York University, and medical and law students from Columbia University). During her third year, Mae was elected president of the Cornell Student Executive Committee. In her fourth year, she was the student representative for Cornell to the Association of American Medical Colleges.

Between her second and third years of medical school, in 1979, Mae received a grant from the International Traveler's Institute for health studies that allowed her to visit and work for eight weeks in Kenya, in East Africa. There she worked with the African Medical and Research Foundation (AMREF), formerly known as the Flying Doctors. Health-care workers in this organization travel to remote parts of East Africa, usually by plane because of inadequate roads. Jemison joined AMREF after it had expanded its work to include making epidemiology studies—health reports on people that include background information about the illnesses they have.

The job gave Mae the opportunity to speak the Swahili language she had studied at Stanford. In the Embu District, near Mt. Kenya, she worked on a community health diagnosis project, assessing the health of local residents by determining statistical information on the height and weight of children, number of people in a household, and their vaccination status. While in Africa, Mae also worked in clinics and hospitals, assisting with surgery. She learned about private clinical health care while staying with a dentist in Nairobi, and helped with community medical projects in the city slum known as Kawangware.

Her work in Africa inspired Mae. She decided she would continue looking for ways to help people in developing countries—poor nations in which people have little industrialization and low standards of living. The following summer, she traveled to Southeast Asia. In Thailand, she and other Cornell medical students volunteered in a clinic in a Cambodian refugee camp. Now a fourth-year medical student, Mae put her expertise to work in the emergency room, where she helped treat people suffering from tuberculosis and dysentery. She also oversaw an asthma clinic there.

Mae considered this work a valuable learning experience—one that she believes she benefited from even more than the people she helped. As she explained in a 1993 interview with Nikki Giovanni for *Essence* magazine:

> I've gotten much more out of what I have done than the people I was supposed to be helping. When I was in the refugee camp in Thailand, I learned more about medicine there than I could have in a lifetime somewhere else. I refuse to think those people owe me any thanks. I got a lot out of it.

In 1981 Jemison graduated from Cornell University Medical College with a doctorate in medicine. Usually the next step in getting a license to practice medicine is an internship, followed by participation in a residency program, in which the doctor specializes in a specific medical area (for example, surgery, pediatrics, or internal medicine). From Mae's travels abroad, she knew she wanted to continue helping people in developing countries; she didn't want to move on just yet to a career in biomedical research. So she applied for an internship in the United States, but made no plans to enter a residency program afterward. She figured that after the one-year internship had ended, she would put her medical skills to work as a volunteer in a less-industrialized area of the world.

After graduating, Mae left New York behind and headed back to California, where she worked as an intern at the Los Angeles County/University of Southern California Medical Center (LAC/USC Medical Center). There she received more medical training, and gained valuable experience in general practice medicine. During that time, she began making plans for the following year, looking into volunteer opportunities. But when the internship at LAC/USC Medical Center ended, Mae had not firmed up her future plans. So she took a position as a general practitioner with INA/Ross Loos Medical Group in Los Angeles, but left that job in December 1982.

The new year of 1983 brought Mae the kind of work she had been looking for—with an organization that shared her goal of helping people in developing nations obtain better health and living conditions: the U.S. Peace Corps.

Founded in March 1961 under the guidance of President John F. Kennedy (term, 1961–1963), the Peace Corps is dedicated to the cause of development around the world. The dedicated staff of volunteers from this U.S. government organization helps teach people living in the hardship of poverty, disease, and war how to improve their lives. Peace Corps volunteers have served in more than 100 developing countries in Africa, Asia, the Caribbean, South America, and elsewhere—helping teach citizens in many different fields, including agriculture, education, health care, business, and the environment.

In 1983, Mae accepted a new challenge—joining the Peace Corps, supervising a staff of medical volunteers in Liberia, West Africa. The Peace Corps was founded in 1961 by President John F. Kennedy, seen here at his inaugural address.

Volunteers typically live and work in a country for two years, sharing their skills to help solve the community's problems

Actually, Mae did not join the Peace Corps as a volunteer. Although she initially volunteered with the organization, she was offered a paid staff position as the Area Peace Corps Medical Officer for Sierra Leone and Liberia, in West Africa. For the next two years, from 1983 to 1985, she supervised medical staff and public medical care, was the primary doctor to the volunteers and embassy staff, and taught volunteer personnel. She managed the medical office, laboratory, and pharmacy, and supervised the training of volunteers. She wrote medical manuals and worked on research projects in conjunction with the National Institutes of Health and the Centers for Disease Control. This work included helping with the develop- ment of a vaccine for hepatitis B (a liver disease), schistosomiasis (a disabling disease caused by drink- ing contaminated water or eating infected snails), and rabies (a potentially fatal virus affecting the nervous system that is passed along through an infected animal's bite).

Living in Africa taught Mae many things about the country, its people, and herself. "I learned a lot from that experience," she explained in a 1992 interview with Ms. magazine. "At twenty-six, I was one of the youngest doctors over there, and I had to learn to deal with how people reacted to my age while asserting myself as a physician."

In her autobiography, Jemison described her experience in Africa and how it changed her:

> I encountered diseases I had only read about in tropical medicine textbooks. I worked with Sierra Leonean physicians and nurses trained in the best schools in England and Germany, but who were at times forced to work with little or no equipment, medication, or supplies. . . .
>
> On call twenty-four hours a day, seven days a week for two-and-a half years, in a place so unforgiving of mistakes, I gained flexibility, knowledge, interpersonal relationship skills, and an appreciation of the chal- lenges life poses to so many people on this planet.

In 1985 Mae resigned from her position with the Peace Corps and returned to Los Angeles, where she had accepted a position as a general practitioner for CIGNA Health Plans of California, a health maintenance organization. Now was the time, she decided, to add to her academic background, in biomedical engineering. So she signed up for graduate engineering classes at night at the University of California, Los Angeles, while working during the day as a physician. At the same time, she kept herself in shape by fitting in time for aerobics classes.

In the fall of that year, Mae also decided to apply for an entirely different kind of career—one that had first captured her imagination when she was a child. Although she had put aside her dream of one day traveling in space, she had never relinquished it. That October, Mae Jemison sent in an application for a position in NASA's astronaut training program, sat back, and waited.

4

THE RIGHT STUFF

❦

THE SPACE PROGRAM that Mae hoped to join in 1985 had been around for more than 25 years. During that time it had undergone many changes.

The National Aeronautics and Space Administration had come about in response to the Soviet Union's successful launch of the satellite *Sputnik I* on October 4, 1957. The American people, horrified to see the small Russian satellite orbiting in the skies overhead had pressed the U.S. government to counter this new, frightening challenge with its own scientific program.

Soon afterward, on October 1, 1958, President Dwight D. Eisenhower established NASA, and the space race between the United States and the Soviet Union began. Tasked with bringing the United States into the space age, NASA soon succeeded in sending its own satellites into orbit and developing manned space flight programs.

The astronauts for the new space program had to meet numerous requirements, including passing rigorous physical fitness and health tests. All had to be certified military test pilots, a restriction that eliminated any women from joining the astronaut ranks since only men were allowed to be military pilots. The first NASA astronauts included Alan B. Shepard Jr., who, on May 5, 1961, flew the first 15-minute suborbital flight, as part of Project

In 1961 Russian astronaut Yury Gagarin (seen here) made history with his orbit of the earth aboard Vostok I.

Mercury. Shepard's flight made him the first American in space, although by then the USSR had already sent the first man into space. Soviet cosmonaut Yury Gagarin had orbited the Earth a month earlier aboard *Vostok I*.

Under the administration of President John F. Kennedy, who took office in 1961, the space race continued. The American government remained committed to the venture, and provided the funding needed for NASA to create major facilities. They included the Marshall Space Flight Center (1959) in Huntsville, Alabama; the Launch Operations Center (1961) in Cape Canaveral, Florida (renamed John F. Kennedy Space Center in 1963); and the Manned Spacecraft Center (1963) in Houston, Texas (renamed Lyndon B. Johnson Space Center in 1973).

On May 25, 1961, President John F. Kennedy set a new goal for NASA of "landing a man on the moon and returning him safely to Earth" by the end of the decade. With the success of the Projects Mercury, Gemini, and Apollo, this dream became reality on July 20, 1969, when *Apollo 11* traveled to the moon and Neil Armstrong and Buzz Aldrin set foot on its surface. Mae Jemison was 12 years old at the time.

Throughout the 1960s, the young girl had watched the television broadcasts of NASA's first tentative steps into outer space—experimental launches, space walks, and spaceship dockings. Seeing these images had helped fuel her desire of one day taking part in space exploration herself. And by the time she graduated from Stanford, in 1977, the space program itself had changed so that its astronauts were not all white males.

After making several successful landings on the moon, NASA had revamped its space program; during the 1970s, it began developing a new type of spacecraft. Known as the Space Transportation System, or STS, the new space shuttle consisted of three parts: an orbiter powered by three main engines, which carried the crew in orbit around the planet; two solid-fuel rocket boosters, which provided initial thrust to the orbiter during launch; and an external tank, which carried the half a million gallons of propellant burned during the first eight minutes of launch.

The new space shuttle was quite different from the Mercury, Gemini, and Apollo spacecraft. To reduce mission costs, engineers had designed a reusable vehicle. Only one of the STS's three components—the external tank—was disposable. Both the solid-fuel rocket boosters and orbiter could be reused. The two solid-fuel rocket boosters would be retrieved from the Atlantic Ocean after dropping off, and then refurbished for the next launch. After returning from space, the orbiter would land like a plane on a runway, either at the Kennedy Space Center or at Edwards Air Force Base in California, and then be quickly prepared for another mission.

During the 1970s, four working orbiters were built for the STS. All were named after pioneering sea vessels used in scientific research and exploration: *Columbia*, *Challenger*, *Discovery*, and *Atlantis*. However, the first space shuttle test orbiter, used in 1977 for aerodynamic testing, was named after a science fiction vessel. It was called *Enterprise*, after *Star Trek* fans mounted a write-in campaign to name it in honor of the television program's starship: the USS *Enterprise*.

As the STS was being developed during the 1970s, a change was taking place in American society. In 1972 Congress had passed an amendment to the Civil Rights Act of 1964, which stated that federal agencies, such as NASA, could not discriminate on the basis of sex, race, religion, or national origin. By the mid-1970s, the space agency began to actively recruit women and minorities as astronauts for the new space shuttle.

Many requirements had changed. Shuttle astronauts did not need to meet the same physical fitness standards established during NASA's early days because the gravity acceleration forces during launch and landing were lower with the orbiter than they were with Mercury, Gemini, and Apollo spacecraft. Height and weight restrictions no longer held. When early astronauts had blasted into space, they had traveled in very small vehicles that limited the allowable height and weight of the occupants. In the much larger shuttle, which carries a crew of six or seven, the only thing affecting the astronaut's size is the ability to fit into the Extra Vehicular Activity (EVA) suit that is worn for space walks. The orbiter provides a comfortable "shirt-sleeve" work environment, so astronauts don't need to wear bulky space suits while inside the ship.

The design of the STS reflected that the purpose of space flight had changed. Engineers created a 15 x 60 foot cargo bay in the 122-foot-long orbiter so that it could carry satellites, telescopes, or scientific equipment—referred to as payload. This feature reflected NASA's new goal: astronauts would work in space by placing payloads into orbit, servicing equipment already in orbit, and retrieving and stowing equipment from space orbit to take back to Earth for repair. The shuttle could carry payloads weighing up to 65,000 pounds for delivery into low Earth orbit, and bring back payloads weighing up to 32,000 pounds.

No longer focused on the goal of placing men on the moon, NASA turned to scientific and technologic research as the main purpose for space flight.

As a result, two kinds of NASA astronaut positions evolved: the pilot astronaut and the mission specialist astronaut.

The pilot astronaut is either the commander of the mission or the pilot of the spacecraft. Like the captain of a ship, the commander is in charge, responsible for the spacecraft, crew, and mission. The pilot, as second in command, operates the shuttle. Pilot astronauts must be U.S. citizens; have at least a bachelor's degree in engineering, biological science, physical science, or math; and have logged at least

In the 1960s, NASA's focus was on reaching the moon. Astronauts like those seen here underwent rigorous testing and training before missions.

1,000 hours flying time in a jet aircraft. There are also strict physical fitness requirements.

The mission specialist astronaut works with the commander and pilot, helping with everyday shuttle operations, such as monitoring the crew's use of fuel, water, and food; conducting experiments; taking charge of payload activities; and participating in space walks. Mission specialists must be U.S. citizens and have fulfilled the same academic requirements as the pilot astronauts—a bachelor's degree in engineering, biological science, physical science, or mathematics—as well as have at least three years of related professional experience.

There is also a third kind of astronaut—the payload specialist—who is not an official member of NASA's astronaut corps. Payload specialists are professionals in the physical or life sciences who are skilled working with equipment unique to the shuttle. They can also differ from pilot astronauts and mission specialists in that they are not necessarily U.S. citizens. For non-NASA programs, these astronauts are usually assigned to a mission because of a payload sponsor or customer. They take the same NASA training courses as the other astronauts to become familiar with shuttle systems, equipment, and procedures. Such training can take as long as two years.

During the late 1970s, as NASA looked to increase its numbers in the astronaut corps, it encouraged minority applicants to apply for positions as pilot astronauts and mission specialists. The first round of new recruits, selected in January 1978, included six women, three African Americans, and an Asian American. Subsequent recruitment efforts brought four more women and members of minority groups into NASA in May 1980. Recognizing the need to maintain a large number of astronauts in

The first African American in space, Colonel Guion "Guy" Bluford flew aboard the space shuttle Challenger in 1983. Subsequent missions included other African Americans: Ronald McNair, Frederick Drew Gregory, and Charles F. Bolden Jr.

the space agency, NASA officials decided to begin reviewing astronaut applicants on a yearly basis, beginning in 1983.

Among the new space shuttle astronauts was Colonel Guion "Guy" S. Bluford Jr., who journeyed on the *Challenger* on August 30, 1983, to become the first African American in space. Other black astronauts included Ronald McNair, who in February 1984 also flew aboard the *Challenger*, following Bluford as the second African American in space. The first African American shuttle pilot was Frederick Drew Gregory, who flew the *Challenger* in 1985. He was followed the next year by African American pilot Charles F. Bolden Jr., who flew the

Columbia. By the mid-1980s NASA was clearly no longer an all-white domain.

However, the fact remained that there were still no African American women in the astronaut corps. Mae Jemison believed she had the ability to change that situation. She once stated that seeing Colonel Guion S. Bluford Jr. travel into space had inspired her to apply to NASA. She had also been impressed by Sally Ride, who in June 1983 was the first American woman in space.

Although no black woman had been selected by NASA to be an astronaut, Mae knew she was well qualified for the job of mission specialist. She held a degree in chemical engineering and a doctorate in medicine, and she had several years experience as a medical doctor. Through years of dance, exercise, and weight training, she carried an ideal weight of 140 pounds on a trim 5' 9" frame. When she sent in her application in October 1985, the timing seemed just right.

But just a few months later, tragedy struck the space program. On a freezing cold morning in Florida, on January 28, 1986, the space shuttle *Challenger* exploded just 73 seconds after its launch. The accident killed the seven *Challenger* astronauts: commander Francis R. "Dick" Scobee, pilot Michael J. Smith, mission specialists Judith A. Resnik, Ellison S. Onizuka, and Ronald E. McNair; and payload specialists Gregory B. Jarvis and Sharon Christa McAuliffe.

While investigators worked to discover what caused the accident and to redesign the space shuttle program, NASA halted its recruitment of astronauts and no space shuttles flew for more than two years. It was ultimately determined that the explosion occurred because of a design flaw in the solid-fuel rocket booster tanks, a failure attributed to faulty O-ring seals joining sections of the right-hand rocket

booster. During the investigation, many people raised concerns about NASA safety standards, which apparently had been compromised because the space agency had been attempting to meet an intensely grueling launch schedule.

After the *Challenger* accident, Mae continued to work at her job with CIGNA Health Plans, but she didn't let go of her dream of becoming an astronaut. The following October, when NASA reopened its astronaut selection process, she submitted another application. Years later, Jemison

January 1986 marked a tragic setback for NASA's shuttle program. Cold morning launch temperatures and failed seals on the shuttle's rocket booster caused a devastating explosion that killed all aboard. Despite the disaster, Mae remained determined to realize her dream of space travel.

would note that the *Challenger* accident didn't frighten her away from wanting to join the space program; instead it made her more determined to succeed as an astronaut. As she explained in a March 2001 online interview, she fully understood the dangers of the job:

> The *Challenger* accident makes us all remember that space exploration with humans is not something to take for granted. But it's not unexpected that accidents will happen—whether in space exploration, underwater exploration, or going into different areas of the world. The important thing is not to take unnecessary risks. You must understand the best you can what problems exist, and figure out how you can get rid of those problems, or how you can develop backup systems. . . . Accidents have happened and will happen. But you don't stop getting into cars just because there was an accident. You just have to figure out ways to make it safer.

Four months after submitting her second application, Mae received word that NASA was definitely interested in her—from a field of about 2,000 applicants, she was among 100 candidates chosen for interviews. The next step required a visit to the Johnson Space Center, in Texas, for a week of tests and personal interviews. Of the 100 aspiring astronauts, NASA planned to select just 15 finalists.

In Houston, flight surgeons evaluated the applicants to make sure they were mentally, emotionally, and physically fit to travel in space. The potential astronauts underwent eye exams, sinus X rays, blood tests, hearing tests, psychological tests, and physical examinations. During Mae's physical exam, the surgeon indicated that Jemison had a heart murmur, a problem that would eliminate her from the program.

Mae explained that when she was at medical school, doctors had detected this murmur and said it was caused by the shape of her chest wall and the heart's position, not by any heart abnormality. A clean bill of health was verified by a follow-up echocardiogram and she stayed in the running.

The U.S. space agency needs its astronauts to be team players, to be able to work well with others, especially during emergencies. Successful applicants to the astronaut corps, according to NASA officials, have to be "highly skilled generalists with just the right amount of individuality and self-reliance to be effective crew members." Mae had to prove to the interviewers that she had the right stuff—that she had not only the right mental and physical qualifications but also the right personality for a NASA astronaut.

After completing the weeklong interview process, Mae flew back home to California to await final word. In the meantime, she and several friends were interviewed by the Federal Bureau of Investigation, as part of a background check. Many weeks later, while at work on June 4, she received a phone call from George Abbey at NASA. In an interview with *Ebony* magazine, she described what happened: "I was sitting at my desk in between patients, and the phone rang, and I was told basically that [NASA] wanted me to come down. I was very happy. I still had to go see patients . . . so I had to hold it in a little bit. I didn't jump up and down and do a dance, but, yes, I was very excited."

At the age of 30 Jemison became the first African American woman ever accepted into the ASCANs (Astronaut Candidates) training program. Her selection brought immediate fame. As the media clamored for interviews with the first black female astronaut, suddenly everyone knew who she was.

5

ASCAN TRAINING

❦

During her one-year basic training program at the Johnson Space Center in Houston, Mae took basic science and technical courses— including mathematics, oceanography, meteorology, guidance, and navigation. She also flew training missions in a T-38 supersonic jet to prepare her for space flight.

IN AUGUST 1987 Mae moved to Houston, Texas, to begin the rigorous one-year basic training program required of all new Astronaut Candidates at the Johnson Space Center. Her fellow ASCANs came from all walks of life, each bringing different skills. She was the only medical doctor. The others were test pilots, a meteorologist, an astrophysicist, a mechanical engineer, and a NASA flight controller.

ASCAN instruction requires at least 60 hours per week of intense mental and physical training. Participants study a range of topics in the classroom and learn various skills while aboard jets and in simulators—mock-ups of the equipment they will use when in space.

In the classroom, Mae and the other Astronaut Candidates took basic science and technical courses, including oceanography, geology, mathematics, astronomy, physics, meteorology, and guidance and navigation. They also learned about the history and hazards of space flight (including a review of the *Challenger* accident), aerospace contractors, and current flight research. There was plenty of information to take in, assimilate, and understand.

Outside the classroom, ASCANs spent much of their time training in a two-seater supersonic aircraft, the T-38 trainer jet. Pilots flew the T-38 to maintain their flying skills, while mission specialists rode in the back and learned about various aspects of jet flight. As a mission specialist, Mae spent a great deal of time in the T-38, where she learned how to handle the radios, fly straight and level, control the plane once off the ground, and plan the flight. She learned how to jump with a parachute and practice survival tactics for use in the wilderness and in the water, skills that would be needed in case of an accident while training on the jet. Mae soon familiarized herself with the requirements of jet flight and aircraft safety, including emergency procedures.

But the job of the mission specialist requires great familiarity with the equipment to be used in space. As Mae explained in a 1989 interview with *Ebony* magazine, "We are the ones people often call the scientist astronauts. Our responsibilities are to be familiar with the shuttle and how it operates, to do the experiments once you get into orbit, to help launch the payloads or satellites, and also do extra-vehicular activities, which are the space walks."

To gain expertise in the workings of the shuttle system, Mae and the other ASCANs attended lectures, sat through briefings, and read textbooks and flight operations manuals. Pilot astronauts practiced in a mock-up of the orbiter flight deck, which contained switches and controls like those in the actual shuttle. Mission specialists worked in a mock-up of the mid-deck, which contained a galley, toilet, sleep station, storage lockers, entry/exit hatch, and air-lock hatch to the cargo bay. There they learned the day-to-day routines of shuttle life, such as housekeeping, maintenance, and waste management and stowage. Using Single System Trainers (SSTs), which feature controls and displays like those in the orbiter, they learned how to operate specific switches and systems and how to respond to malfunctions in a shuttle environment.

Mae also practiced in the Shuttle Mission Simulator (SMS), a mock-up of the shuttle that was developed in 1977 to train shuttle crews on procedures beginning at 30 minutes before launch. Built at a cost of about $1 million, the SMS consists of two orbiter cockpits, one configured just for the use of the shuttle commander and pilot and the other for the use of the commander, pilot, mission specialist, and payload operations crew. The SMS allows mission specialists to practice procedures involving navigation, rendezvous, use of the remote manipulator (robot arm), and payload facilities.

ASCAN training provides not only the tools for astronauts to practice with but also the environment they will encounter when in space. Because learning to perform tasks in a weightless environment is a top priority, NASA has developed two ways to provide a weightless environment for astronauts.

One method requires the "neutral buoyancy trainer," a large, 25-foot-deep tank of water, also referred to as the Weightless Environment Training Facility (WETF). The huge tank can hold a full-scale mock-up of the orbiter payload bay and air lock. The ASCANs, wearing pressurized EVA suits, are neutrally buoyant in the water—they neither float nor sink—which allows them to get a feeling of what it is like to work in the cargo bay or make space walks while weightless.

Astronauts also practice in actual weightlessness, achieved during free fall aboard a specially modified four-engine transport jet, the KC-135. The plane follows a parabolic flight path, swooping up and then down, much like a car on the steep hills of a roller-coaster ride. After the plane reaches the top of a loop, free fall occurs for 20 to 30 seconds during the downward plunge, making the jet's occupants weightless. For those brief moments, while they float about, they can practice using a piece of shuttle equipment

Working in the weightlessness of space requires special training. Jemison (right) and her fellow crewmembers trained underwater in special suits and aboard a modified KC-135 airplane that simulates zero-gravity by flying in steeply curving climbs and dives.

or simply become comfortable with moving around, eating, or drinking. A training exercise might include as many as 30 free-fall sessions.

Mae completed her ASCAN training in August 1988, and received the special pin commemorating her official membership in NASA's astronaut corps. As she explained, the ASCAN training had involved not only learning new concepts but also making good friends: "By the end of our first year, when we all received our astronaut pins, we had learned tons about spacecraft, orbital dynamics, planetology, and how the human body adjusts to weightlessness, aerodynamics, the space shuttle, NASA—and each other." Mae was the fifth black astronaut and the first black female astronaut in NASA.

Jemison's first NASA position was as an astronaut office representative at the Kennedy Space Center at Cape Canaveral, Florida. The timing was good, for NASA was about to resume its space shuttle program, which had been canceled for more than two years because of the *Challenger* accident. On September 29, 1988, the successful launch of the *Discovery* heralded a new beginning for NASA's STS program, and many more shuttle launches soon followed. One of Mae's jobs was to help process the shuttles before launch (checking payloads, shuttle heat-resistant tiles, and countdown). She also worked in the Shuttle Avionics Integration Laboratory (SAIL), where she verified shuttle computer software.

It would not be until May 1991, however, before a replacement shuttle for the *Challenger* joined NASA's fleet. Like the space orbiters before it, the new shuttle, the *Endeavour*, was named after a sailing ship used in early exploration, in this case the ship commanded by 18th-century British explorer James Cook. The *Endeavour* received its name through a national competition held in U.S. elementary and secondary schools. Unlike the other three orbiters, however, this spacecraft contained equipment with more advanced technology and could support longer missions—of up to 28 days duration.

Astronauts usually become eligible for a flight assignment one year after completing basic training, although some have waited as long as five years before being assigned to a space shuttle flight. At the time they join NASA, astronauts sign a contract stating they will work with the agency for several years so that it can benefit from the time invested in their training.

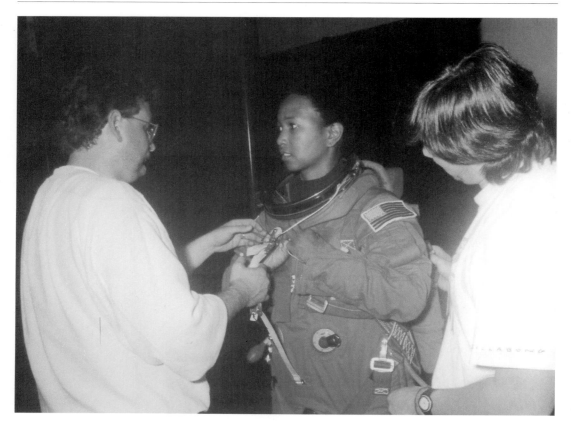

In 1989 Jemison learned of her assignment to the newest shuttle, the Endeavour, *whose scheduled 1992 mission would involve conducting scientific experiments in space.*

Mae had to wait only one year before learning in 1989 that she was assigned to the payload crew of the newest space shuttle, the *Endeavour,* as part of mission STS-47 Spacelab J. This was a cooperative venture between NASA and the National Space Development Agency of Japan (NASDA); the "J" in Spacelab J stands for Japan. Initially scheduled to launch in the summer of 1992, the mission involved conducting experiments in materials science (including areas such as biotechnology, electronic materials, fluid dynamics, glasses and ceramics, metals and alloys) and the life sciences (including areas such as human health, development biology, animal and human physiology and behavior, and space radiation).

These experiments would be conducted in space, aboard the *Endeavour* in a reusable, modular laboratory known as Spacelab J. Designed to fit into the payload bay of any of the four space shuttle orbiters—the *Discovery, Atlantis, Columbia,* and *Endeavour*—the spacelab is a 23-foot-long pressurized structure built by the European Space Agency (ESA). NASA considered the scientific mission of great significance because it would establish a relationship between two of the nations—the United States and Japan—involved in plans for an international space station. Astronauts from the European Space Agency and Canada would fly on similar research missions.

Training for mission STS-47 soon began. Because Japan was providing many of the experiments that would be carried out on the flight, Mae spent more than two years training there, learning how the experiments should be run and how to use Spacelab J. During that time, she also become proficient in speaking Japanese.

After some schedule changes, the launch date for mission STS-47 was set for September 12, 1992.

6

ABOARD THE *ENDEAVOUR*

❦

Six TALENTED CREW members accompanied Mae on her historic flight on the *Endeavour*. Its commander, navy captain Robert L. "Hoot" Gibson, was traveling in space for the fourth time. He held a bachelor of science degree in aeronautical engineering from California Polytechnic State University. His pilot was air force colonel Curtis L. Brown Jr., who had a bachelor of science degree in electrical engineering from the U.S. Air Force Academy. The shuttle's 50th mission was Brown's first flight in space.

Air force colonel Mark C. Lee was serving as payload commander, responsible for the planning and coordinating of payload and space shuttle activities while the craft was in orbit. Lee held a bachelor of science degree in civil engineering from the U.S. Air Force Academy and a master of science degree in mechanical engineering from Massachusetts Institute of Technology.

Mission STS-47 was Lee's second flight, although his presence and that of mission specialist N. Jan Davis made for another significant first. When the *Endeavour* launched on September 12, 1992, it was carrying the first married couple into space: Lee and Davis had both flown on previous missions, but this was the first time the two were flying together. Davis had entered the astronaut

The only medical doctor onboard, Jemison was well trained in performing complex experiments in zero-gravity conditions.

69

program with Mae in August 1987. She had a bachelor of science degree in applied biology from Georgia Institute of Technology and a doctorate in mechanical engineering from the University of Alabama in Huntsville.

Also on his second flight was mission specialist Jay Apt. He had a bachelor of science degree in physics from Harvard College and a doctorate in physics from Massachusetts Institute of Technology. As flight engineer, Apt was responsible for operating the orbiter during his work shift on the shuttle.

NASDA astronaut Dr. Mamoru Mohri, on board as a payload specialist, became the first Japanese astronaut in space when the *Endeavour* reached its orbital path. The Japanese citizen had a bachelor and master of science degree in chemistry from Hokkaido University, and a doctorate in chemistry from Flinders University of South Australia. Jemison, Davis, and Lee had all trained with Mohri in preparation for mission STS-47 Spacelab J.

Once the *Endeavour* was established in its orbit, payload commander Mark Lee activated the spacelab module in the payload bay so the astronauts could set to work immediately. They had much to accomplish. In order to run experiments around the clock, the crew worked two 12-hour schedules, referred to as the Blue and Red shifts. Along with Jan Davis and Jay Apt, Jemison worked the Blue shift, which coincided with nighttime hours in the United States. Mark Lee and Mamoru Mohri were on the daytime hours of the Red shift, along with the commander and pilot.

During the flight, Jemison and the other astronauts transferred between the bus-sized space lab and the pressurized crew compartment by floating through an eight-foot-long, 40-inch diameter, pressurized tunnel. This passageway allowed the crew members to remain in a pressurized environment as they moved between the orbiter mid-deck and the spacelab module.

Spacelab J carried 44 experiments designed by researchers in Japan and the United States—24 materials science projects and 20 life sciences experiments. Many of these experiments dealt with the effect of microgravity, or low gravity. With the materials science projects, scientists wanted to see how low gravity affected the manufacture of drugs, metal alloys, and electronic components. With the life sciences experiments, mission specialists planned to document how humans, plants, and small animals developed and adapted to microgravity. In addition to the Spacelab J experiments, the *Endeavour* also carried other self-contained experiments in special canisters.

Although Mae has admitted that being able to float was one thing she particularly enjoyed on her space voyage, weightlessness actually creates many problems for astronauts. The human body is physiologically affected by weightlessness: muscles can atrophy (deteriorate), space travelers suffer from motion sickness, minerals leach from the bones, and there is a reduction in the rate of bone formation. Although these effects can be reversed when the astronauts return to Earth, NASA researchers hoped some of the STS-47 Spacelab J experiments studying the effects of microgravity on people and animals could help provide ways to counteract the adverse effects of weightlessness.

Scientists already knew from previous space flights that exercise helps prevent muscle atrophy. To keep the body from "deconditioning," NASA researchers recommended that astronauts perform at least 15 minutes of daily exercise to keep the muscles, including the heart, strong. Exercise equipment on the *Endeavour* included stationary bikes, which as Mae has said gave the astronauts the opportunity to bicycle 260 miles above the Earth, but going nowhere at all. Still, they knew that regular exercise would help reduce muscle atrophy and make the readjustment to Earth's gravity much easier when they returned home.

The *Endeavour*'s crew performed the following life sciences experiments during the mission to help researchers to evaluate other adverse effects of weightlessness, including motion sickness, mineral loss, and slowed bone formation.

Biofeedback Experiment: About half of the astronauts who travel in space suffer from motion sickness, with symptoms ranging from sinus congestion, headache, and fatigue to loss of appetite, nausea, and vomiting. Researchers have discovered that certain medications can help astronauts overcome symptoms of motion sickness. NASA wanted to develop other methods to counteract motion sickness symptoms that didn't require using medicine.

Mae participated in a three-day experiment aboard the *Endeavour* in an attempt to discover whether biofeedback, a method of self-calming involving meditating or deep-breathing exercises, could help space travelers cope with motion sickness. Instead of taking drugs when she felt symptoms coming on, Mae used biofeedback techniques to gain control over what are usually involuntary bodily responses (such as heartbeat and respiration). She had learned these techniques during training on a simulator at the Marshall Space Flight Center, where she had learned how to control her body's reaction to the stresses of spaceflight.

Mae's partner, Jan Davis, did not receive biofeedback training. As part of the experiment, both astronauts wore portable equipment that measured their physiological responses during the first three days of flight, except when sleeping.

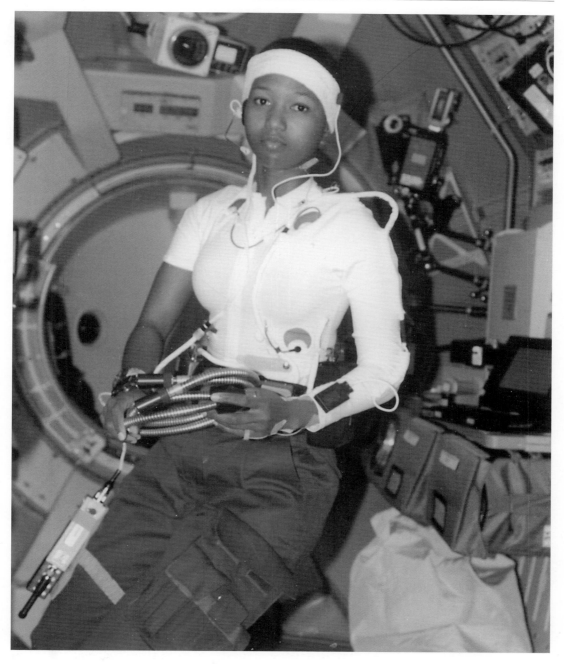

Aboard the Endeavour, *Jemison was fitted with devices that monitored her ability to reduce the adverse symptoms of space flight using biofeedback, a technique of meditation and breathing exercises.*

Mae wore a special shirt that allowed electrodes to be attached to her torso and a headband with an instrument that measured her head movements. A ring measured blood flow and skin temperature, while another instrument worn on her wrist monitored her pulse. An instrument in the belt she wore around her waist recorded data. Researchers at NASA's Ames Research Center planned to analyze all of this information at the mission's end. After the three-day experiment was completed, the monitoring experiment was put away.

As it turned out, using biofeedback to calm herself whenever symptoms of motion sickness set in worked for Mae. However, as she noted later, because so few people participated in the experiment, it is not clear whether medication or biofeedback was the more effective technique for dealing with motion sickness.

Bone Cell Research (BCR) Experiment: As a coinvestigator of the Bone Cell Research experiment, Mae performed an experiment aimed at determining the effects of microgravity on bone growth. Jemison worked with rat bone cell cultures, which reproduce more quickly than human cell cultures. Using a microscope equipped with a 35-mm camera, Jemison first took pictures of two sets of cell cultures; then with a syringe she withdrew the old media (or food) from the cultures and injected one set of cells with nutrients only. The other cell culture received the same nutrients, but was also injected with a special parathyroid-related protein. Parathyroids, or endocrine glands in the thyroid, make a hormone that affects the formation of calcium, the mineral that makes bones hard. Meanwhile, at the Kennedy Space Center on Earth, Dr. Nicola Partridge of the St. Louis School of Medicine conducted a similar experiment so that investigators could compare the data obtained on Earth with that gathered by Jemison in microgravity.

When in space, humans undergo demineralization—they lose more calcium from their bones than they lose when on Earth. Demineralization causes a loss of bone density, weakening the bone and making it susceptible to fractures, much like the disease osteoporosis. Bone demineralization could create a serious problem for the crew members during long space missions, such as those that were being planned for the international space station.

Research done at the time of Jemison's flight had shown that the longer women stay up in space, the more calcium they lose, and they lose it faster than men do. As Mae explained in a 1992 interview with *Ms.* magazine, "Women are more prone to osteoporosis, and black people tend to have heavier bone skeletons than whites, but we don't have a lot of data on women. . . . The real issue is how to keep people healthy while they're in space." It was hoped that NASA's ongoing research in this area would not only help astronauts on the future international space station but also result in the development of methods or medications that could help patients with osteoporosis on Earth.

Chicken Embryo Development Experiment: Another experiment that took place on the *Endeavour* evaluated the bone and muscle development in chicken embryos during space flight. The mission specialists observed various stages of growth of 30 fertilized chicken eggs. By observing this embryonic development in space, it was hoped that researchers could learn why bones become weaker and lose calcium when in low gravity and to learn how bone formation changes during space travel.

The fertilized chicken eggs, which were kept at a constant temperature in a thermoelectric incubator in the orbiter mid-deck, had to be rotated, much like a hen on Earth moves her eggs during the chicks' development. Jemison and Davis were responsible for rotating the eggs during their crew shift. NASA researchers planned to examine the eggs after the *Endeavour* returned to Earth—some immediately to determine bone formation, while the rest would be allowed to develop to maturity. Scientists at NASA were very interested to see what effect, if any, the weightlessness of space might have on future development of eggs.

Frog Embryology Experiment (FEE): Mae worked on another experiment that investigated the effect of microgravity, but this time on the development of frog eggs. In the course of this research, frog eggs were laid, fertilized, and hatched in the microgravity environment of space for the very first time.

To begin the experiment, Jemison injected four female frogs with a hormone that caused eggs to be shed. Later, while working in a special enclosed compartment for handling the specimens, she selected two sets of eggs and, using a microscope equipped with a video camera to observe the process, fertilized the eggs.

Half the fertilized eggs were kept at microgravity, while the other half were spun in a centrifuge that simulated normal Earth gravity. During the days that followed, Mae, and a team of investigators at Ames Research Center who watched via video camera, looked for any differences in how the tadpoles developed in their skeletal, muscle, and nervous systems. Using a formaldehyde mixture, Jemison stopped and preserved various stages of growth of some of the frog eggs (these preserved specimens were to be studied later).

Mae also documented her observations of the

swimming behavior of tadpoles that had been hatched before launch. Of particular interest was tadpoles' development of the inner ear balance system, or otolith, which affects spatial orientation. Members of the FEE research team on Earth also made observations using the microscope's video camera.

During their mission, Endeavour's crew had to work closely with in the confines of the shuttle. This group portrait shows the crew in their zero-gravity environment.

Subsequent results showed that both sets of tadpoles—those raised in microgravity and those in artificial Earth gravity—grew normally, and with no defects. Both also showed similar swimming behavior. These results suggested that weightlessness caused no problems in tadpole development and adaptation to microgravity. Later, the tadpoles were returned to Earth where they developed normally into adult frogs.

Testing of the Lower Body Negative Pressure (LBNP) System: On Earth, body fluids such as blood flow throughout the entire body. However, in the weightless environment of space, body fluids stay in the upper part of the body. This effect does not create a problem for the astronaut when he or she is traveling in space; however, upon returning to the normal gravity of Earth, the sudden loss of blood flow to the brain can cause dizziness and fainting, a condition known as orthostatic intolerance. There is also concern that because of this effect, the cardiovascular system is weakened.

In conjunction with Dr. John Charles and his team at NASA's Johnson Space Center, Davis and Jemison tested an instrument that could help astronauts prevent this adverse effect and readapt more easily to Earth's gravity. Known as the lower body negative pressure (LBNP) instrument, the device consisted of a fabric, cylindrical bag that seals around the waist. A pump lowers the pressure in the system, thus applying negative pressure that forces fluids back into the lower extremities during a 30-minute period of decompression.

Jemison and Davis took turns using the system and monitoring the subject's physiological responses. As part of this research, they performed echocardiographic scans (ultrasound measurements) of the heart and recorded heart rate, blood pressure, and leg volume measurements. Previous use of the LBNP system during earlier missions showed that the effectiveness of the treatment lasted for up to 24 hours.

Testing of the Fluid Therapy System: On Earth, patients in need of fluids can receive them from intravenous (IV) drip systems. However, IV administration needs gravity to make fluids flow down from the IV bag into the body. In the low gravity environment of space, this method of storing and administering medication does not work.

Recognizing that astronauts might need fluid infusions during long missions in space, medical researchers developed an alternative system that uses a pump instead of gravity. Jemison and Davis tested this fluid therapy system using a medical training mannequin arm, which featured veins and a solution reservoir, as their "patient." After mixing various solutions, they filled several IV bags, then infused the solutions by pump into the mannequin arm. At the same time, a similar procedure was performed at the Kennedy Space Center, with the plan to later compare the data, as well as the actual mannequin arms, for quantity and quality of the fluids administered.

Although most of the astronauts' time on the *Endeavour* was filled with working on experiments, they also had free time to relax, listen to music, or read. Some of the space travelers also took time to keep people back on Earth informed about what they were doing.

On the fifth day of the mission, Davis and Jemison took a break from their busy schedule to participate in televised interactive programs being broadcast from the shuttle. Speaking in Japanese, along with Mamoru Mohri, Jan and Mae discussed weightlessness and life on the shuttle with students from Mamoru's former junior high school in Hokkaido. Later, Mae spoke with a group of students, teachers, and community leaders gathered at

In an important onboard experiment, Jemison tests an intravenous fluid pump system designed for medical use in zero gravity.

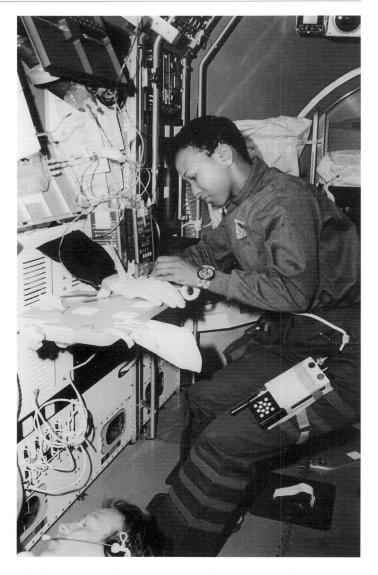

the Museum of Science and Industry in her hometown of Chicago. During her presentation, she credited her teachers from Morgan Park High School as a great influence on her and her choice of a career. She also enthused about the scientific work taking place on the *Endeavour*, describing Spacelab as a "very successful mission."

That prediction would prove correct, as by the time mission STS-47 had ended, its crew had managed to collect data for all the experiments carried out on board the *Endeavour*.

7

BACK TO EARTH

—— ❦ ——

BECAUSE THE *ENDEAVOUR* crew conserved its consumables (resources such as food, fuel, and oxygen) so well, NASA managers had extended the length of the mission by an additional day. By the time the orbiter touched down on Kennedy Space Center Runway 33, at 8:53 A.M. on Sunday, September 20, its crew had spent more than 190 hours in space and circled the Earth 127 times. In other words, the *Endeavour* had traveled more than 3 million miles around the planet.

Dressed in their blue NASA G suits, the exhilarated crew members emerged from the ship, smiling at the success of their mission. After routine medical examinations, the seven astronauts headed back to Houston, where colleagues and friends greeted them. One of the many interviews that Mae gave was to her best friend from Stanford University, Linda Lorelle, who, as the NBC-KPRC Houston evening news anchor, was covering the event.

As she stood before the group, Mae shared her thoughts about her historic flight: "Was I excited? Yes. Did I have a good time? Definitely. Is it something I'd do again? In a heartbeat."

In the months following Mae's return to Earth, she was interviewed by reporters for numerous magazines and newspapers. In these interviews Mae took the opportunity to speak her mind about the

After more than 190 hours and 127 earth orbits, the Endeavour *touched down safely at Kennedy Space Center. As the first African American woman in space, Jemison quickly became something of a celebrity, with reporters from various magazines clamoring for interviews.*

role of black women in the space program. In December 1992 she told *Ebony* magazine that she hoped many more women of color would soon follow in her footsteps and that she hoped her example would educate society about how astronauts can and should be women and members of minority groups: "People don't see women—particularly black women—in science and technology fields. My participation in the space shuttle mission helps to say that all peoples of the world have astronomers, physicists and explorers."

In an interview with *Ms.* magazine, she added to these thoughts: "More women should demand to be involved. It is our right. This is one area where we can get in on the ground floor and possibly help to direct where space exploration will go in the future."

Many of the mementos that Mae had taken along with her on her journey into outer space reflected these beliefs, as well as Mae's own interests, hobbies, and pride in her African-American heritage. Among the items Jemison carried on the *Endeavour*'s September flight was a banner of the black sorority Alpha Kappa Alpha, of which she was an honorary member; a Michael Jordan Chicago Bulls jersey; and a statuette from West Africa. She had also brought proclamations from the Chicago Public School System and from the DuSable Museum of African-American History, as well as a poster advertising the Alvin Ailey American Dance Theater's performance of *Cry*—a dance that portrays the trials of African American women.

In a 1993 interview with *Essence* magazine, Jemison explained why she chose the specific items she carried with her on the *Endeavour:* "I wanted everyone to know that space belongs to all of us. There is science in dance and art in science. It belongs to everyone. I'm not the first or the only

African-American woman who had the skills and the talent to become an astronaut. I had the opportunity. All people have produced scientists and astronomers."

Jemison had acquired many honors before her history-making flight, given in recognition of her selection as an astronaut. In 1988, she had received the *Essence* Science and Technology Award, and the following year had been named the Gamma Sigma Gamma Woman of the Year. In 1991 *McCall's* included her on its list of the 10 Outstanding Women for the '90s. In early 1992, the Detroit, Michigan, Public School System named an alternative public school after her—the Mae C. Jemison Academy. Mae had carried a banner from the school with her on the *Endeavour*.

Many more honors and awards followed when Mae returned from her flight. In 1992, her hometown of Chicago celebrated her 36th birthday as part of a six-day, citywide tribute on October 17. During the celebration, Jemison visited Morgan Park High School, where she addressed the students who had packed into the school auditorium. In her speech, she recalled the kindergarten teacher who had puzzled over Mae's desire to become a scientist, and she urged the students not to be limited by others' preconceived notions about them. At another event at the DuSable Museum of African-American History, she received a commemorative photograph of the first black woman aviator, Bessie Coleman, from Coleman's niece, Miriam Coleman.

Later that year, the DuSable Museum of African-American History celebrated its 30th anniversary by presenting History Maker Awards to Chicagoans who had made significant contributions to society, the city, or the nation. The special posthumous awards went to journalist and civil rights activist Ida Bell Wells and Chicago mayor Harold Washington,

Following in the tradition of the first black woman aviator, Bessie Coleman (seen here in 1923), Jemison encouraged others to break through societal barriers and achieve their dreams.

while living recipients were Mae, along with film-maker Robert Townsend, civil rights leader Rev. Jesse L. Jackson, and publishing entrepreneur John Johnson.

In 1993 Jemison received recognition as one of *Ebony* magazine's 50 Most Influential Women. That same year *People* magazine honored Mae Jemison as one of the "50 Most Beautiful People in the World," and she was also inducted into the National Women's Hall of Fame.

In the spring of 1993, Mae was the subject of a Public Broadcasting Service documentary: *The New Explorers: Endeavour*. The film covered her story as an astronaut in training, and included background information supplied by her parents. In the documentary, Mae's mother explains the key to her daughter's success: "We were taught that education was everything, which is what we taught her." The documentary also describes Jemison's experiments aboard the *Endeavour*, and ends with her joyful visit to her Chicago high school.

Earlier in the year Mae had taken a leave of absence from NASA to teach a course, "Space Age Technology and Developing Countries," at Dartmouth College, in Hanover, New Hampshire. The break from the routine as a NASA astronaut helped Mae make what she later referred to as "a most difficult personal decision." It was time to make a career change.

In March 1993, Mae Jemison resigned from her position with NASA, after having spent six years as an astronaut. Her training manager for the *Endeavour* mission, Homer Hickam, believes she left because the astronaut job emphasized too much specialization. "Mae's personality was too big for that," he said. "I see Mae as a sort of all-around ambassador. She just really wanted to make a connection with the world."

MEETING A MENTOR

Shortly after Mae became an astronaut and began working at the Kennedy Space Center, she heard Nichelle Nichols being interviewed on the radio. Many years had passed since the actress first gained fame on the television series Star Trek, *yet her celebrity as Lieutenant Uhura remained strong. During the late 1970s Nichols had helped NASA recruit women and minority members to the astronaut program. Through public service announcements and personal appearances, she reached out to many prospective Astronaut Candidates who otherwise might not have applied to NASA, knowing of its history of hiring only white males.*

Now, in 1987, the actress was in Orlando, Florida, helping to publicize a Star Trek *convention. Mae immediately headed off for the convention, where she identified herself to the security guards for Nichols and asked to be introduced to her. Although strangers, the two women embraced at their first meeting, perhaps in recognition of both having been the first to brave new frontiers.*

Nichols and Jemison subsequently became good friends. Although a family illness prevented Nichelle from attending the Endeavour's *launch on September 12, 1992, the two women spoke together on the phone the night before. Later that year, during the 14th Annual American Black Achievement Awards, Nichols presented Jemison with the Johnson Publications Company's Black Achievement Trailblazer Award, for becoming the first black woman in space.*

In May 1993, Mae had the opportunity to become a part of Star Trek *lore herself when she appeared in the highly popular syndicated television series* Star Trek: The Next Generation. *The longtime* Star Trek *fan had jumped at the offer to play a small part on the show. She appeared in the episode "Second Chances" as Lieutenant Palmer, a woman on transporter room duty.*

*Jemison explains that the influence of the popular science fiction program did more than provide a valuable role model for her as a young girl. The stories on the program itself moved her because they presented a future in which all kinds of people, regardless of gender, race, or ethnicity, worked together in space. "Here was affirmation," Jemison recalled in her autobiography. "*Star Trek *immediately captured my imagination and respect. Amid the scares of nuclear proliferation and annihilation, moral and ethical conflicts concerning criminal justice, nationalism in colonies, the second and third waves of racial riots in the United States, and the promise of uncertainty of physical science advances,* Star Trek *presented a hopeful view of humanity and the future."*

In the NASA press release announcing her resignation from the astronaut corps, Mae explained that she planned to pursue interests in "teaching, mentoring, health care issues and increasing participation in science and technology of those who have traditionally been left out." She added, "I leave with the honor of having been the first woman of color in space, and with an appreciation of NASA—the organization that gave me the opportunity to make one of my dreams possible. The experiences of the NASA astronaut program have opened many doors, and provided a way to put my hard work and training to use for the good of others." Indeed, Mae had new goals in mind, and a desire to contribute to people around the world.

8

NEW ENDEAVORS

✤

For Jemison, the honors and awards keep coming. In 2001 she received an honorary Doctor of Science degree from Rutgers University President Francis Lawrence.

AFTER LEAVING NASA, Jemison became a full-time professor at Dartmouth College in the Environmental Studies Program. She also became very involved in developing ways to help less-industrialized countries use technology to improve the living conditions of their citizens. One of the first organizations that she founded and now directs is the nonprofit Jemison Institute for Advancing Technology in Developing Countries.

The Jemison Institute, based in the Environmental Studies Program at Dartmouth College, involves faculty and students at the college as well as the schools of engineering, medicine, and business. The organization works to research, design, implement, and evaluate technology to determine its value for use in developing countries.

According to the Jemison Institute website, the organization's mission is "to ensure that the benefits of the world's technical advances contribute to the well-being of the more than seventy-five percent of the world's people living in developing countries." Projects include energy development initiatives between the United States and countries in Africa, and S.E.E.ing the Future (Science, Engineering, and Education). During the S.E.E.ing the Future forum held in the fall of 2000, under the auspices of the National Science Foundation, participants evaluated the role of public funding in engineering technology and scientific research.

Jemison strongly believes in sustainable development—what she has described as "improving human quality of life now such that the ability of future generations to grow and prosper is not compromised." Mae thinks that technology must be used to improve the way of life for not only those in wealthy, industrialized nations but also people in poorer countries. In other words, technology should be available for everyone, and in areas such as health care, food production, infrastructure, environmental safety, manufacturing, social services, and ecosystem preservation. To achieve these goals, the Jemison Institute works in partnership with other universities, as well as industry, governments, agencies, foundations, and businesses throughout the developing and industrialized world.

In the summer of 1994 Mae founded the for-profit technology-consulting firm, Jemison Group, Inc., located in Houston, Texas. The company researches, develops, and markets advanced technologies, especially those that improve communications and health care for people living in western Africa. Many of its employees have worked in the design and flight operations of the U.S. space program.

The Jemison Group is developing a satellite-based telecommunication system, called Alafiya, to facilitate health-care delivery in the developing world. Alafiya, which means "good health" in Yoruba (the language spoken in the West African nations of Nigeria, Benin, and Togo), is being used in remote areas of Africa to help prevent illness, foster public education, and allocate health-care resources.

The company is also working on ways to store energy and make it easily available in developing countries. Among the solutions under development are solar-thermal electricity-generating systems that can store power for nighttime use and during periods of heavy demand.

Another goal of the Jemison Group is to promote science education and literacy. This is being achieved by various projects, including the introduction of U.S. science and literature curricula into South Africa and the establishment of The Earth We Share (TEWS), an international science camp founded and directed by Jemison that emphasizes critical thinking and a hands-on, or experiential, curriculum.

The Earth We Share is run by the Dorothy Jemison Foundation for Excellence (DJF), an organization established in memory of Mae's mother and the teaching ideals she stood for. Dorothy Jemison taught in Chicago Public Schools for 25 years and had passed along to her daughter the principles of maintaining "personal excellence" in work and activities. The DJF strives to help children grow up to become adults who contribute effectively to their society.

Mae feels strongly about fostering a love of science in young people, and The Earth We Share is designed to do this. The four-week residential program brings together students, ages 12 through 16, from countries around the world. The camp's location changes from year to year; various school and college campuses from across the United States have hosted the summer program. The first TEWS camp was held in July 1994 and included 27 students from Nigeria, Sierra Leone, Sweden, Trinidad, and the United States who attended the camp at Choate Rosemary Hall, a preparatory school in Wallingford, Connecticut. Subsequent locations have included Camp Algonquin, in Algonquin, Illinois; Talladega College, in Talladega, Alabama; Dartmouth College; and Willamette University, in Salem, Oregon.

TEWS tries to utilize the natural curiosity of children, teaching them to make connections between society, science, and technology. During the camp, students working in teams of eight to ten are presented with a problem, usually a contemporary global issue, about which they must determine a solution, carry out that solution, and then evaluate the results. The website for The Earth We Share lists some of the thought-provoking problems addressed by previous camp participants: "What to do with all this garbage?" "Design a crime control system for the year 2005." "Design the world's perfect house." "How many people can the Earth hold?"

Other features of TEWS camps include student-run radio program broadcasting, astronomy education, participation in team or individual sports, guest lecturers, field trips, and sharing of cultures.

In June 2000 the program hosted an event entitled, "The Earth We Share 2000: Preparing the World for the Next Century," which was based in Chicago. It included a 24-hour International Youth Internet Conference, during which young people from all over the world were invited to come up with ways to solve the world's most pressing environmental and social concerns. Greene Elementary School, of the Chicago Public School System, served as the world headquarters for the ambitious project.

Jemison commented on the TEWS 2000 event: "It's only fair that we give today's students a chance to express their views about the world they'll be inheriting very soon. Then it's up to us adults to take note—and action." Muhammad Ali joined the students during an hour of the 24-hour Internet conference, which included questions such as "Whom do you trust most to solve global problems in the next 25 years?" and "What are the most difficult challenges you may face in the next 25

years?" During TEWS 2000, the winners of an international essay contest on shaping the world were announced; submissions had been received from schools in Ghana, Portugal, China, India, the United States, and Australia.

Mae has found other ways to encourage young people to learn more about what science has to offer. When her schedule permits, Jemison visits schools to talk to students, with the intent to

As founder of The Earth We Share (TEWS) program, Jemison hopes to pass on her legacy to a new generation of young scientists. At a recent TEWS event, former heavyweight boxing champ Muhammad Ali (seen here) joined students for an hour of the 24-hour internet conference.

inspire them with the love of learning she herself grew up with. She also speaks at various schools as Bayer Corporation's National Science Literacy Advocate, a position she has held in the company's "Making Science Make Science" program since 1995. The program encourages hands-on, inquiry-based science learning, employee volunteerism, and public education.

In her position as a science literacy advocate, Mae travels with Bayer executives around the country, speaking with individuals and before groups, spreading the word about the need for quality hands-on, inquiry-based science education. Jemison has met with thousands of individuals, including principals and school district administrators and federal, state, and local government officials, as well as parents, students, and teachers.

Jemison has also shared her interest in science by reaching television viewers. From 1994 to 1995 she hosted a weekly television program entitled *World of Wonder*, which was featured on the Discovery Channel. She worked as a technical consultant for the series as well.

Because of her role as the first black woman in space, Mae received several honorary doctorates from institutes such as Lincoln College, in Pennsylvania, and Winston-Salem State University, in North Carolina. Her work since that time has also earned her recognition, with the receipt of an honorary doctorate bestowed by Princeton University, in New Jersey.

Mae has served as a member on a number of boards, including the National Research Council's Space Station Review Committee and the board of directors of Spelman College, a private liberal arts, historically black college for women located in Atlanta, Georgia. Jemison has also served on the board of directors of Scholastic, Inc., the Keystone

Center, and the National Urban League. In January 1999, a Presidential Ballot national straw poll conducted by the White House Project selected her as one of the top seven women leaders.

Mae is a popular speaker, both nationally and internationally, at many professional meetings and college and university commencements, where she often addresses the need for more science literacy and increased women and minority participation in math and science education. In 1996 she gave a graduation address at the 105th commencement of her alma mater, Stanford University, where she urged the new graduates to acknowledge the need to cooperate and work together with people regardless of race, religion, or ethnicity.

In a talk delivered at Oklahoma State University in 1999, she spoke from her own experience of the importance of choosing one's future wisely:

> It was my right and responsibility to live up to my potential, to my ambitions. This is my one life, this is my journey. I had to learn very early never to limit myself because of someone else's limited imagination.
>
> There are 86,400 seconds in each day. Each one of those seconds is extremely precious, because we can do with each of those seconds exactly as we please, but we can never get a single one of those seconds back. But I can guarantee, if we use our seconds, choosing the future that [we] want, then we will each have a lifestyle that we desire.

In 1999 Jemison returned to Cornell, having accepted an appointment as the President's Council of Cornell Women Andrew D. White Professor-at-Large. The following year she delivered a speech as part of the 10th anniversary celebration of the President's Council of Cornell Women. During her talk, Mae stressed that science needed to be put to

Jemison remains firmly committed to inspiring young minds. In her work with students she stresses the importance of breaking barriers and creating a future as limitless as our imaginations.

use to help improve the world, that choices in energy use, pollution, and food distribution should be made so that people can "survive as a species the way we want to live on this planet without destroying its ability to sustain us." That same year she was inducted into Stanford's Black Community Services Center Black Alumni Hall of Fame.

Many people consider Jemison a powerful role model for girls and African Americans, although she prefers that others not try to copy what she has done in life. Rather, she encourages students to find their own path. As she advised in an interview with *Ebony* magazine, "Don't try to necessarily be like me or live your life or grow up to be an astronaut or a physician unless that's what you want to do. The thing that I have done best throughout my life is to do the best job I can and to be me." Both her example and speeches reflect a determination that science-related studies and careers be open to all, and she encourages women and minorities to pursue careers in science or in the field of their choice.

Years after her historic flight, Jemison continues to be honored for that achievement. In the spring of 1997 the newly built Museum of African-American History opened its doors in Detroit, Michigan. Inside the 120,000-square-foot building, eight room-size exhibits portray African-American history and culture from the 14th century to modern times. Among the modern artifacts in the permanent exhibition is the flight suit worn by Dr. Mae Jemison when she rode into history on the *Endeavour*.

When Mae is asked to identify the people who have made the greatest impact on her life and life choices, she points to those who helped and taught her while she was growing up—her parents, aunts and uncles, friends, teachers, and neighbors. But she also mentions someone she never met—Linus Pauling—who won the 1954 Nobel Prize in chemistry and the 1962 Nobel Peace Prize for his campaign against the use of nuclear weapons. Jemison admires Pauling as a scientist who helped her know the importance of exploration and discovery, and also of social responsibility.

Mae lives in a small southeast Houston suburb with her cats, including Sneeze, whom she adopted while living in West Africa. In her spare time she enjoys reading, and considers fiction, science fiction, and adventures as her favorites. She keeps in shape with jazz dance, exercising, lifting weights, and playing volleyball and likes to spend time cooking, watching movies, and traveling. When asked in an online interview about her future plans, the former astronaut demurs, noting,

When asked about her greatest influences, Mae is quick to mention Linus Pauling, winner of the 1954 Nobel Prize for chemistry and the 1962 Nobel Peace Prize for his campaign against the use of nuclear weapons.

"It's tough to think that far ahead. . . . One of the things I hope to be doing is still dancing, being healthy, and learning new things."

In March 2001, Mae Jemison published an autobiographical memoir—*Find Where the Wind Goes: Moments from My Life*—in which she tells anecdotal stories about events in her life, from childhood until the point when she left NASA. She wrote the book, she once explained, "because I wanted to let people know about the importance of continuing to journey through life. . . . There are lessons all along—you can pay attention or not. But there are always hints about being in the world and doing what you want." She added, "One of the best stories that I've heard is that we're all on this spaceship Earth. As passengers, we need to pay our fare. So, we should understand what kind of contributions we can make to this world. They're different for every person, but we should make sure that we pay our fare."

Mae Carol Jemison is one determined passenger on planet Earth who has paid more than her fare, following her dreams and giving her skills and expertise to make major contributions to the nation and the world. With her passion and compassion for humanity, her drive and commitment to be all she can be, this pioneer in space flight has accomplished a great deal in exploring other new frontiers in her effort to bring science and technology to everyone in the world.

CHRONOLOGY

1956   Mae Carol Jemison born on October 17 to Charlie and Dorothy Jemison in Decatur, Alabama

1959   Jemison family moves to Chicago, Illinois

1973   At age 16, Mae Jemison graduates from Morgan Park High School in Chicago; enrolls at Stanford University, Stanford, California

1977   Graduates from Stanford with a bachelor of science degree in chemical engineering; fulfills requirements for bachelor of arts degree in African and African American studies

1981   Graduates from Cornell University, New York, with a doctorate in medicine degree

1982   Interns at Los Angeles County/University of Southern California Medical Center; serves as general practitioner with INA/Ross Loos Medical Group in Los Angeles, California

1983   Serves as medical officer for Peace Corps in Sierra Leone and Liberia, in West Africa

1985   Works as physician for CIGNA Health Plans of California in Los Angeles; applies to NASA's astronaut program

1987   Is one of 15 applicants (out of 2,000) accepted into NASA's astronaut program

1992   Becomes first black woman in space in flight on space shuttle *Endeavour*

1993   Resigns from NASA; becomes professor at Dartmouth College, where she teaches environmental studies; founds and becomes director of the Jemison Institute for Advancing Technology in Developing Countries

1994   Founds and becomes director of the Jemison Group, Inc., in Houston, Texas, and The Earth We Share, an international science camp

1995   Becomes Bayer Corporation spokesperson

1999   Accepts appointment as the President's Council of Cornell Women Andrew D. White Professor-at-Large at Cornell University

2001   Publishes memoir, *Find Where the Wind Goes*

BIBLIOGRAPHY

Books and Periodicals

Bolden, Tonya. *And Not Afraid to Dare*. New York: Scholastic Press, 1998.

Carreau, Mark. "Shuttle Glides to Safe Landing, Ends Joint Mission with Japan." *Houston Chronicle*. 21 September 1992, p. 5.

"The 50 Most Beautiful People in the World." *People Weekly*. 3 May 1993, p. 145.

Giovanni, Nikki. "Shooting for the Moon." *Essence*. April 1993, p. 58.

Graham, Judith, ed. "Mae C. Jemison." *Current Biography Yearbook 1993*. New York: W. Wilson Co., 1993.

Haynes, Karima A. "Mae Jemison: Coming in from Outer Space." *Ebony*. December 1992, p. 118.

Hodges, Ann. "Out of This World/Mae Jemison Inspiring in 'New Explorers.'" *Houston Chronicle*. 3 May 1993, p. 1.

Katz, Jesse. "Shooting Star: Former Astronaut Mae Jemison Brings Her Message Down to Earth." *Stanford Today*. July/August 1996.

Marshall, Marilyn. "Child of the '60s Set to Become First Black Woman in Space." *Ebony*. August 1989, p. 50.

———. "Close-Up: A New Star in the Galaxy." *Ebony*. December 1992, p. 122.

Smith, Jessie Carney. *Notable Black American Women*. Detroit: Gale Research, 1992.

"Space Is Her Destination." *Ebony*. October 1987, pp. 93–96.

Yannuzzi, Della A. *Mae Jemison: A Space Biography*. Berkeley Heights, N.J.: Enslow Publishers, 1998.

BIBLIOGRAPHY

Websites

Dr. Mae C. Jemison
   [http://www.dartmouth.edu/~jemison/JI_profile.html]

Dr. Mae Jemison's Official Home Page
   [http://www.maejemison.com]

The Earth We Share (International Science Camp)
   [www-theearthweshare.org]

The Jemison Institute
   [http://www.dartmouth.edu/~jemison/]

The Johnson Space Center
   [http://www.jsc.nasa.gov]

The Kennedy Space Center Space Shuttle Mission Chronology
   [www-pao.ksc.nasa.gov/kscpaol/]

Live Interview with Mae Jemison
   [http://teacher.scholastic.com/space/interview/tscript.htm]

NASA Quest: Female Frontiers—Mae Jemison
   [http://quest.arc.nasa.gov/space/frontiers/jemison.html]

National Women's Hall of Fame
   [http://www.greatwomen.org/jemison.html]

Selection and Training of Astronauts
   [http://liftoff.msfc.nasa.gov/academy/astronauts/training.html]

FURTHER READING

Buchanan, Doug. *Air and Space*. Female Firsts in Their Fields. Philadelphia: Chelsea House Publishers, 1999.

De Angelis, Gina. *The* Apollo I *and* Challenger *Disasters*. Great Disasters: Reforms and Ramifications. Philadelphia: Chelsea House Publishers, 2001.

Jemison, Mae. *Find Where the Wind Goes: Moments from My Life*. New York: Scholastic Press, 2001.

INDEX

INDEX

INDEX

INDEX

PICTURE CREDITS

LEEANNE GELLETLY is a freelance writer and editor living outside Philadelphia, Pennsylvania. She has worked in publishing for more than 20 years; this is her second book for Chelsea House.